BMW
CARS

MARTIN BUCKLEY
PHOTOGRAPHY BY NICK DIMBLEBY

MBI Publishing Company

First published in 2001 by MBI Publishing Company, Galtier Plaza, Suite 200, 380 Jackson Street, St. Paul, MN 55101-3885 USA

MBI Publishing Company books are also available at discounts in bulk quantity for industrial or sales-promotional use. For details write to Special Sales Manager at Motorbooks International Wholesalers & Distributors, Galtier Plaza, Suite 200, 380 Jackson Street, St. Paul, MN 55101-3885 USA.

Library of Congress Cataloging-in-Publication Data Available

ISBN 0-7603-0921-3

Edited by Kris Palmer
Designed by Tom Heffron and Stephanie Michaud

Printed in Hong Kong

On the front cover: Few corporations have been more acutely aware of their heritage than BMW. For years they have milked esteemed older models like the 328 and 507 for every ounce of publicity value. They wasted no time in posing the new Z8 flagship supercar with the "Oldtimers."

Endpapers: The 2800 saloons were aimed directly at Mercedes and were outstanding cars. The styling struck just the right note of modern, airy good taste.

On the title page: The 507 was BMW's most dramatic flagship model since the 328, though it was more of a profile-raiser than a true production car—only 253 were built. Using the fairly pedestrian 502 saloon chassis in shortened form BMW clothed it in a roadster body of outstanding purity.

On the back cover:
BMW's Turbo 2002, 2002, and 2002 cabriolet.

The M coupe of 1997 won the approval of the press and looked more purposeful than the roadster but has yet to grab the attention of buyers.

The 600 was a four-seater alternative to the Isetta introduced in 1957 and was a step toward a "real" car although it still looked rather like an Isetta and retained the front door arrangements.

CONTENTS

There is an appealing and popular version of BMW's history. It runs like this: Amid the economic devastation wrought by World War I, the company struggles to harness a skilled Bavarian work force to produce cars alongside aircraft and motorcycles. It begins with a humble Austin Seven built under license but quickly moves forward to produce outstanding cars like the 328, only to fall victim, once again, to war and destruction. Literally reborn from the ashes on the strength of enthusiasm, it struggles to produce stylish and ambitious luxury vehicles in the face of extreme economic hardship. When solid profits fail to materialize, the Quandt family and a loyal band of owners and dealers rescue the struggling company from the jaws of receivership. Saved

BMW has one of the best-organized heritage collections and has had an excellent museum since the early 1970s. Few other companies were taking their past quite so seriously in those days. Their mobile museum—*BMW Mobile Tradition*—is a collection of running, driving exhibits that can be tested by journalists.

The big 501 and 502 saloons of the 1950s tend to be dismissed by historians of the marque, but they were important in getting the company back on its feet again, and they were fine, luxurious cars in their day.

The 2002 was a massive hit across Europe and North America and did more than any other car to establish BMW as a force in the performance-car market. It was the father of the 3 series.

from extinction once more, BMW refines its engineering genius and perfectionism to produce the *neu classe* sedans of the early 1960s. Through their design and engineering superiority, this line of cars forms the basis for an unstoppable success story in subsequent decades.

Like all popular histories, this version has elements of truth within it. Yet it fails to credit the company fully for the vision and creativity it had from the start. Our argument is that BMW has been, from the outset, a curiously modern company—ahead of its time not in terms of the technology employed in its vehicles, nor in the methods of production adopted, but in the way the company operated and related to the particular economic landscape in which it was situated.

First and foremost, it was a business. It did not operate as a workshop turning out cars, but as an entity engaged in the process of generating profits. Instead of following the markets, BMW shaped and molded them. Instinctively strategic in all its thinking and responses,

BMW reflects unique features of the German economy and state and also wider facets of economic life. In this sense it was, from the first, both a modern company and an international one. Paradoxically associated with one region more closely than virtually any other automobile manufacturer—perhaps because its home is part of its name?—BMW's products and thinking were truly global.

Economic devastation and war were not random accidents that befell the company. Its customers were as much the state and military authorities as the wider public. This diversity and focus as a business rather than as a workshop accounts for some of the company's success. However much the kidney-shaped radiator may express continuity and tradition, this was an unsentimental company. Flexible and pragmatic, it drew on particular traditions of German business for its leadership style. This was not a company shaped and guided by dominant and willful engineers like Issigonis, Porsche, or William Lyons, with their own particular foibles and

preferences to accompany their special talents. Instead the figures guiding BMW in the early years had something of the flamboyance of the wealth of their age.

Any history that claims to provide answers is suspect. Instead the historian's task is to point up possible lines of inquiry, show different ways of understanding the seemingly familiar and settled. It often seems that the more convincing and seamless an account of any human endeavor appears, the further it is likely to be from the reality. This trend makes us look again at the 328

and its awesome reputation and to question the established accounts of BMW's revival in the early 1960s.

Readers of this book are likely to be enthusiasts of BMW cars. Very probably they will own, or aspire to own, desirable examples of what has been regarded for several decades as a premier sporting marque. A proper celebration of the marque requires not just an appreciation of the undoubted technical qualities of the cars, but also an understanding and assessment of the very distinctive achievement of this most modern of companies.

As a road car, the American-built X5 is regarded as the best of the current crop of SUVs (sport utility vehicles) and is an amazingly good machine for what is, after all, BMW's first off-road 4x4.

CHAPTER 1

THE CREATION OF A "MODERN" BUSINESS IN A TURBULENT ERA

Previous page: The 328 made its debut in 1936 at the Nurburgring, where driver Ernst Henne ran away from the entire grid to win the race. Developed from the unexciting 315 and 319, the 328 boasted hydraulic brakes and knock-off steel disc wheels. This one belongs to American collector Jim Smith of California.

To get into the small-car business quickly, Eisenach took up a license for the production of Britain's Austin Seven. The car that emerged in 1927 was this Dixi 3/15. One hundred Austins had initially been brought to Germany for tests and the setting up of production machinery.

BMW's unique history is often presented along with a diagrammatic "family tree." This is no surprise. BMW has a complex genealogy that perhaps owes more to the nature of German industrial and economic life than to the character of any individual involved. Many manufacturers grew through the leadership of a single forceful personality focused on fixed goals and possessed of simple, competitive reflexes. BMW was, and is, a more complex creation.

From its earliest days, BMW has been a shifting portfolio of businesses, plants, and products. Acquisition and divestment have been regular features of its growth and development. From its earliest days it has exhibited the kind of features that we think of as marking out the "modern" company. Whatever the outward appearance, it has proved to be uninhibited by tradition, rational in its calculation, flexible and unsentimental in its choices and strategy. Its history provides a contrast to many vehicle manufacturers who have exhibited more headstrong and romantic approaches to their business.

BMW was a business first, and a car manufacturer second. As a business the skills that were essential to its success were an ability to connect with and respond to the market. At various times in its history it did not display these skills to great effect. Various models didn't sell well, and it went through a distinctly shaky period in the 1950s. Yet, on balance, it is the one manufacturer that stands out for its ability to sense the direction in which spending power and fashion were moving and to build upon those shifts.

A close look at its history reveals something else. To succeed, any auto manufacturer must develop and refine the skills of designing and building cars. But it is not those skills that separate the history of BMW from that of many long-forgotten carmakers. Instead, it is BMW's skills in marketing, in building a brand, and developing an aura and reputation around its products. The company's skill in negotiating the twists and turns of economic fortune as deftly as it shaped its products makes this manufacturer remarkable.

To understand the early history of BMW, one must appreciate the economic climate in which it grew. The market for industrial goods in the first half of the twentieth century in Germany bore little resemblance to the simple fiction encountered in economics textbooks. While the appearance may have been a plethora of independent companies competing for the attention of free consumers in the marketplace, the reality was different. In the world in which BMW operated, the customer was often the state or the military. Relations with competitors

A familiar profile on the roads of Britain in the 1920s and 1930s and, indeed, for many years afterward. The company built 6,182 of these German versions to December 1928, and it only differed from the English Austin Seven in its badging. The BMW-badged 3/15 with four-wheel brakes was introduced the following year.

were part competitive, part collaborative. Extensive mutual cross directorship and interconnection between companies was a feature of the German industrial landscape. So also was the active involvement of the banking sector in industrial entrepreneurship—brokering deals and providing managerial input, with a long-term perspective quite alien to practices in the United States and the United Kingdom.

For much of the period, the state and the military were key shapers of the market for German industry. BMW grew primarily by relating to this market, and its pre–World War II car production was shaped by the ebbs and flows of military and state contracts. These contracts, despite their ebbs and flows, insulated BMW from total dependence upon a fickle consumer base. They gave BMW the resources and confidence to develop cars alongside its core business in airplane engine and motorcycle manufacture. Government contracts were important, not just because they were profitable. In the aeronautical field, they financed the development of

metallurgical advances and production methods that could be translated into the car production at little cost to the firm. Similarly the range of government contracts supported a network of suppliers and subcontractors already connected to the company with whom it could work on automotive developments.

The reality of German rearmament was far from a smoothly managed venture. Each of the armed services pursued its own program of growth with little regard for the others. Projects were delayed, went over budget, and were poorly controlled. For manufacturers involved, this could be frustrating but also profitable. BMW as an enterprise learned early to cope with this environment and to manage it to its benefit.

The first cars carrying the BMW name appeared in 1928. They were modified Austin Sevens built under license from Herbert Austin. BMW, as a company, was by that time a well-established airplane engine and motorcycle manufacturer, formed by the amalgamation of two existing airplane engine manufacturers in 1921.

Their movement into car production was effected by the simple expedient of acquiring an existing respected, although financially marginal, manufacturer, Dixi Automobiles. An existing Dixi product, the Austin Seven built under license, was rebadged as a BMW, and the existing BMW motorcycle sales network was encouraged to promote the vehicles. It was a simple, pragmatic way of securing entry into the rapidly developing car market.

The Austin Seven had already proved a highly successful vehicle, bridging the gap between motorcycle and full-size car and bringing motoring to those who had to count carefully the cost of their journeys. It was simple and achieved acceptable performance and good economy by virtue of its light weight. Versions were built under license by a number of manufacturers, most notably Rosengart in France. By the time BMW became involved in its production, the Austin Seven had already been on the market for some years and outlived the hordes of cyclecars that had emerged in the 1920s.

The Dixi-Austin (DA1), as it was called, had slowly been improved with the addition of front brakes and increased power. It emerged under the BMW name as the 3/15 in 1929 and sold in reasonable numbers. Over 12,000 were produced between the summer of 1929 and the spring of 1931—to put the operation in perspective, Opel produced nearly four times as many examples of its comparable 4/20 model during the same period.

The earliest days of BMW car production are illustrative of the way German industry operated. The acquisition of the heavily indebted Dixi company by BMW arose through interconnected directorship. Dixi had been amalgamated with the Goathaer Waggonfabrick AG sometime earlier by financier Jakob Shapiro, whose business portfolio included both enterprises. Shapiro's connections with BMW also made it possible for him to later engineer a takeover by BMW that had mutual benefit. BMW's diverse business activity gave it greater stability than Dixi, which was purely an auto manufacturer. Shapiro, closely connected with the company, knew of BMW's desire to enter the automotive market as soon as possible. BMW's purchase of Dixi demonstrated the characteristically pragmatic business style that was to shape the company's future. Similarly it illustrates the way German banking institutions sought to preserve their long-term interests. The German banking industry preferred to strengthen weak companies through amalgamation, rather than dismantle them to recover their asset value.

BMW's 3/15 was built on a production line of sorts, while previous Dixi products were created in more

traditional ways. A variety of body styles were offered—a sedan, two-seat cabriolet, four-seater convertible, and even a delivery van. A number were supplied to the Reichwehr, and several hundred were supplied in chassis form to specialist coach builders who built bodies to their own design to enhance the appeal of the small car. Around 150 small, sporty two-seaters, based on the familiar 3/15 chassis, were also built and designated the DA3 (the Wartburg name was resurrected to apply to them). These tend to feature strongly in the histories of BMW, though they probably had little impact on the fortunes of the firm.

The economic climate of the late 1920s and early 1930s was bleak, with a dramatic drop in world trade. Yet different sectors of the market were affected in different ways, and the motor industry was very much more insulated from the economic disruption than were other older, established industries. In Germany, BMW felt the effect of a government cutback on airplane projects, yet the small car continued to sell well in a market expanding with customers conscious of the small Austin-based product's economy. And the company's chosen product areas—aeronautics and motor vehicles—were sectors of the economy that all could see were likely to grow rapidly

The interior shows that this was no-frills transport for the masses. The irony of BMW's takeover of the Rover Longbridge plant (once the home of Austin) in 1994 was not lost on historians.

One of the staples of BMW's prewar production was the six-cylinder 309 and its successor, the 315, both relatively undistinguished cars of straightforward design that were clothed in various sports, saloon, and even van bodywork. This is the four-window tourer 309, owned by American enthusiast Tom Graham. The 309 was originally sold in the United Kingdom as a Frazer Nash BMW, Frazer Nash having the concession for the marque before the war.

in the near future. Moreover, they were sectors of the economy in which the state was keenly interested. BMW had sufficient confidence in the future and in its product to invest also in the French Rosengart version of the Austin. BMW also developed its substantially modified version, the DA4 (or BMW 3/20), that featured a rather poorly thought-out swing axle suspension, and quickly canceled its license agreement with Austin.

The 3/20 was thought of at the time as a limousine in miniature. Tastes, however, change. Look at it today and it seems overbodied and to have lost something of the simplicity that was the attraction of the Austin Seven. It was developed at the Eisenach works, where the Dixi company had produced its first cars, under the Wartburg brand, in 1899. The 3/20 used an overhead valve engine and had swing axle suspension front and rear, along with a backbone chassis. The specification was more modern than its predecessor, but the resulting vehicle had its failings. Its portly all-steel body may have been attractive to purchasers at the time, but the car weighed over 330 pounds more than the DA2. Performance and economy both suffered. The swing axle suspension also left a lot to

be desired. At that time the key issue for suspension designers was not road-holding, handling response, or even ride quality, but the ability to minimize the shake and shimmy that infected vehicle steering. The 3/20 suspension system provided poor wheel location and was prone to generate powerful resonance and vibration on certain road surface conditions.

It would be wrong to imagine that these technical failings determined the success of the 3/20. Then, as now, most customers have little point of comparison for their purchases and, of course, BMW's competitors were not without their weak points. Sales were lower than for the previous model, with only 7,500 produced before the model was withdrawn in 1934. This is more likely to reflect the depressed economic climate of the day than any customer resistance to the particular model. Interestingly the body for the 3/20 was built by Daimler-Benz in its coach works near Stuttgart, reflecting the close connections between the two companies.

Within a year or two, German nationalism and political confidence had taken a new turn. Political forces were attacking the economic depression with active state

action and the motor industry had a part to play in this plan. While on the one hand increased interest in airplane developments was benefiting one part of BMW, the building of the autobahn was a clear positive signal for the auto manufacturing side of the business. Growing middle class incomes underlined the potential of car manufacture in the future, and in 1933 BMW showed a new and more attractive model known as the 303.

Built around a tubular frame and a six-cylinder version of the 3/20's overhead valve engine, the 303 featured the twin kidney-shaped grilles that would become BMW's trademark for the future. A competent and conventional car of the period, the 303 used a rigid rear axle and independent front suspension with a transverse upper leaf spring and bottom A-arms. In appearance the 303 was nicely proportioned. Only 1,200 cc, the six-cylinder engine offered limited performance and consumed more fuel than its four-cylinder predecessor. Bodies were built initially by Daimler-Benz. An outwardly similar four-cylinder model, designated the 309 with an 845-cc engine, was also introduced. Various body styles were available, including some elegant cabriolets. Later in the model run the bodies were built by Ambi-Budd, the German joint venture licensee of the American Budd system of building welded steel bodyshells. It was the introduction of this U.S. system that was to transform the ability of the European motor industry to develop high-volume output.

Commercially, the 303 and 309 were not particularly successful, with only a couple thousand of the six-cylinder machines produced. By 1934 the 303 was phased out and replaced by a larger 1,500-cc-engined model designated the 315. The capacity increase, achieved by using the pistons from the small 309 four with a new long-stroke crank, made the car a rather more competent performer, while detail changes to the chassis gave better ride and handling. Included in the model range was the more sporting 315/1 roadster. With skirted rear wheels and flowing lines, the 315/1 styling reflected the increasing interest in "streamlining" that gave rise to many manufacturers producing "airflow" models. Only around 250 of the sporting 315/1 were produced but they performed well in competition. BMW motorcycle star Ernst Henne scored several successes with the new model.

At the same time BMW was developing these cars, Germany itself was changing rapidly, with increased emphasis being placed on state activity and national confidence. BMW benefited from the increased aircraft production that accompanied these developments. BMW also

An English-registered 315 Tourer. This model used a 1500 engine and had a respectable top speed of over 70 miles per hour.

A grid of 328 roadsters at the Nurburgring in July 1938.

shared to an extent in the government's concerted attempts to promote positive images of both German products and the German nation through sporting activity. BMW motorcycles were very well established in competition, and the 315/1 had clear sporting potential. It played a part in beginning to define BMW as a marque with sporting appeal. That appeal was considerably enhanced in 1935, when the company introduced a larger-engined version, designated the 319/1. It was externally very similar to the smaller engined car, but the extra capacity of the long-stroke engine made it significantly livelier. Once again it was not produced in large numbers. Only 100 were made in total, and it carried a large price tag. The engine was a conventional modern pushrod overhead valve unit without the acclaimed alloy hemispherical head that was to feature in the later 328.

Once again the government's economic and military policies fostered these technical developments. The new German confidence was linked with modernity. Germany wished to place itself at the forefront of technical development, and motors cars and aeronautical engineering held a key part in the German leadership's vision of the future. Working hand-in-hand with manufacturers, the government responded to their requirements rapidly. The country's road network was overhauled, with significant state expenditure on autobahns and resurfacing. The link between engine capacity and vehicle taxation was abolished, offering manufacturers freedom from the sorts of taxation formulas that constrained engine development elsewhere in Europe. The promotion of motorsports through subsidies paid to Mercedes and Auto Union is well known, but other manufacturers benefited

from tax concessions available for investment made to support competition. Much of BMW's competition activity in the late 1930s was at the behest of the NSKK, the Nazi sports movement. The NSKK, for example, commissioned and entered 328s at Le Mans, as well as the special bodied 328s in the 1940 Mille Miglia.

Perhaps more significant still was government intervention and coordination in "rationalizing" and shaping the output of an organization of suppliers. On the one hand, the clear motivation for such initiative was the desire to provide the Nazi military machine with the kind of industrial infrastructure that it required. Yet such a reading of the events owes more than a little to hindsight. The task force entrusted with this rationalization, under the leadership of Colonel Adolf Von Schell, was working not just with military concerns in mind. Within the grips of a corporate ideology, it saw a significant role for the state in reordering the irrationalities of the marketplace on behalf of wider economic and social objectives.

The evidence only allows us to speculate about the consequences of these actions. Yet the concerted attempt to rationalize and integrate the component industry, alongside the stable conditions provided by massive rearmament and associated development, could be seen as positively affecting component supplier quality. People interested in the origin of the engineering quality for

which BMW and the rest of the German motor industry came to be known would do well to look at this period, when component suppliers were encouraged to work together to common standards.

The mid-1930s also marks a turning point for BMW in the sense that a coherent marketing strategy begins to emerge, reflecting the increased affluence of German society. BMW began to plan cars catering to a more discerning market and carrying larger price tags. Sports models, elegant sedans, and stylish cabriolets came to prominence in the model range. Now fitted with larger engines, they offered the power necessary to exploit the new road network, along with the prospect of better unit margins for the business. We should see in this, as in everything done by BMW, a calculated commercial decision, rather than a by-product of the enthusiasm of particular engineers, however attractive such a view might be to the enthusiast.

The most obvious evidence of this shift in focus was the development of the 326. A large sedan with a 113-inch wheelbase, it was the first four-door offering from BMW. Abandoning the less substantial tubular chassis that featured in earlier models, the 326 had a massive box section platform, along with a neat torsion bar–controlled rear live axle. At the front there was the familiar transverse spring and wishbone arrangement, though now arranged with the spring forming the bottom link.

The 328 has a reputation out of proportion to the number built—461—but there can be no doubt that it was an influential car that remained a successful racer even in the 1950s. The shape allegedly influenced William Lyons when he styled the Jaguar XK120.

CAMILLO CASTIGLIONE

Castiglione was a key figure in the early development of BMW. Born in Trieste, he took up Italian citizenship after World War I. A flamboyant figure, he developed an extensive portfolio of industrial and financial interests in Austria, Germany, and throughout the Balkans. He effectively controlled the Austrian aircraft industry in its early years, but his endeavors crossed national and industrial boundaries. A sometime press baron, he helped organize the Salzburg Music Festivals, and he accumulated an extensive art collection. He was head of the Vienna Bank Association and invested heavily in many early aircraft and motor companies, brokering deals between them and guiding their fortunes with a keen eye on the need to extend his own.

It was Castiglione, who through his involvement with Austro-Daimler, encouraged the Austrian government to place an order for airplane engines with the fledgling Bayerische Flugzeugwerke AG, which was to eventually develop as BMW. Throughout the interwar period, he brought business opportunities to BMW and profit to himself. Castiglione sought unsuccessfully to bring BMW into automobile manufacture on a number of occasions. He used his contacts with Austro-Daimler to attempt to get BMW involved in the production of the Sascha car designed by Ferdinand Porsche. Although this plan failed to come to fruition, Castiglione negotiated a subsequent deal some years later that brought the Dixi company into BMW's grasp.

Once again, rack-and-pinion steering was used, though with lower gearing than on earlier, lighter models. Mechanically the car used the familiar 2.0-liter six, though with a further 1-millimeter bore increase giving a capacity of 1,971 cc. The overall styling by Peter Schiamanowski resulted in an elegant, well-proportioned car, which was to be BMW's most popular prewar model. It appeared in various guises. Autenreith of Darmstadt provided two- and four-door convertibles alongside the sedan bodies by Ambi-Budd. BMW made more than 15,000 before halting production in 1941.

Alongside the 326, in 1937 the company briefly offered a hybrid model designated the 329. It combined the mechanics and chassis of the earlier 319 with the front bodywork of the new 326. The origin of this curiosity lay in the shortage of production capacity for the new chassis frame. Once this had been overcome, the 329 disappeared, to be replaced by a further hybrid—the 320. This model used a shortened, modified version of the 326 platform with the older 319 suspension. Powered by a single-carb version of the 326 engine, the 320 was made until 1938, with around 4,000 produced. Once again the origins of these hybrid models lay in the

concern to maximize profitability by utilizing existing production facilities and materials.

In 1936, the company introduced not only the 326 but the famed 328 roadster. The 328 presents a particular problem for the BMW historian. There is no shortage of testimony on the charms of the car. With its streamlined body shape, lusty performance, and good road manners, it has secured pride of place in every account of prewar sports car development. In particular, its competition success is frequently alluded to. There exists an overwhelming consensus that this was a path-breaking car with great influence on the subsequent fortunes of BMW. Given its reputation and subsequent influence, it comes as a shock to find that fewer than 500 were made in a production run beginning in February 1937 and ending in 1941.

Engineered by Fritz Fiedler and Alex von Falkenhausen, the 328 was developed quickly using existing BMW components and technologies. While it may be a car dear to the hearts of enthusiasts, the 328 was no flight of fancy by designers. Like all BMWs, its character and specification were rooted firmly in commercial considerations. The simple large-tube ladder frame was easy and cheap to make, while the use of existing suspension and steering from the 315 and 319 range cut development time and kept costs down.

The only surprises are to be found in the complex and widely acclaimed alloy cylinder head that was grafted onto the existing iron 1,971-cc engine block from the 326. Once again hindsight plays its part in how this engine is viewed. We know that it was developed postwar into a highly successful competition unit used extensively in single-seaters well into the 1960s. We know also that it was highly regarded when installed in Bristols and ACs nearly a quarter century after its initial development. It is not difficult to make a case for it as one of the "great" engines of the period. At a time when competition engines where frequently supercharged, here was an engine that produced power by means of a high-efficiency hemispherical combustion chamber and good porting. With its beautifully finished cam covers reminiscent of a double overhead cam setup, topped off with three big downdraft carbs, it was a beautiful sight for any enthusiast to behold.

Yet the complexity of the valve gear, however beautifully executed, is a result of an attempt to adapt an existing block for new purposes. Certainly the engine proved capable of being developed to produce ever-higher outputs, but much of this increase came from improved fuels allowing higher compression ratios. These developments do not, in themselves, offer testimony to the greatness of the engine. Similarly we should not underestimate the extent to which the performance of these engines coincided with rapid advances in production processes and metallurgy emerging from airplane engine development. As an airplane engine manufacturer, BMW was in a good position to bring these advances to bear on the development of the 328 engine. The subsequent history of the engine with its postwar development by Bristol also involved close contact with airplane engine metallurgical and production expertise. You could argue plausibly that the engine's deficiencies were masked by rapid improvements in metallurgy.

Of course those who argue that the 328 was a milestone in sports car development often support their position by calling it the first vehicle to offer refinement and comfort along with sporting performance. There is substance in this claim. The formula of a rigid chassis and compliant suspension, which is the route BMW took, was relatively unusual for sports cars of the period. Most combined harsh springing with chassis flex, which was a recipe for a lack of refinement. To drive such cars quickly often required strength as well as alertness. The BMW

was certainly more forgiving and refined, yet with fewer than 500 produced, direct experience of the model's qualities would seem inadequate to account for the status that the 328 has acquired. Perhaps we should remember that harsh springing and a flexible chassis may have been characteristic of traditional British sports cars, but it was a recipe that had been challenged by manufacturers such as Lancia from a much earlier period.

Why is it that a sports car produced in such small numbers can have such a hold on enthusiasts who are unlikely ever to have driven one? Of course vehicles are highly regarded in enthusiast circles, and often develop

At the heart of the 328 was a complex six-cylinder engine with hemispherical combustion chambers. The intake valves were operated conventionally by pushrods and rocker arms, and the exhaust valves by a set of 90-degree rocker arms on the same shaft that transferred motion to the cross-rods. A 2.0-liter unit, it developed 80 horsepower.

Not so well known is the 327, a sports version of the 326 built with coupe and cabriolet bodywork of great elegance. BMW produced 1,396 of the model until as late as 1941, along with a much rarer (569 built) 327/28 model that had the cross-pushrod engine of the 328. This car belongs to American collector Jim Smith.

enduring reputations among those who may never own them, for a variety of reasons. How many people would recall the Volvo P1800 if it had not starred in a TV series? Put an E-type alongside its contemporaries and you cannot fail to recognize its charismatic shape and understand its reputation. Listen to any of the large supercharged sports cars of the 1930s and you get some sense of their attraction. But the 328 was not a car of that kind. It was pretty, fast, comparatively refined, but lacked the obvious charisma that would lodge it in enthusiasts' hearts in normal circumstances.

Of course there is the question of competition success. Even before production models had been released, the 328, in prototype form, had secured competition success. The factory motorcycle racer Ernst Henne won a race at the Nurburgring as early as June 1936. This was to be followed by innumerable outright and class victories in all sorts of competition. Important though these victories may have been in bringing the 328 to public attention, one should be careful not to exaggerate their significance. Firstly, most of the victories that the 328 secured were class victories, often against quite weak or outdated opposition. Secondly, whatever benefits accrued to BMW from its motorsport its success must be seen in the context of a period when fellow German manufacturers, Mercedes and Auto Union, were completely dominating European Grand Prix racing.

Mercedes and Auto Union brought to European racetracks dramatic multicylinder supercharged cars of great technical complexity. These machines both demanded and revealed great skill in those who drove them. Worthy though the victories of the little 328 were in the realm of sports car racing, they were no match for the excitement generated by the rivalry of these Grand Prix monsters.

Where the 328 did score was as an accessible sports car that could combine everyday use with successful weekend competition. In this guise it proved a popular point of entry into motorsport for many drivers over a prolonged period. Stirling Moss was only one of many for whom a 328 provided race experience in the early stages of his career. It is the longevity of its presence on the racetracks, as much as anything else, that might account for its status. Look at sports car grids in club racing in the mid-1950s anywhere in Europe and you'll still find 328s present and performing well. Yet is this not just a testimony to its supposedly advanced concept and features? It is as much, if not more, the inevitable effect of wartime disruption and postwar shortage. The 328 was, after all, the most recently developed major sports

car to be introduced before war engulfed Europe. It represented the pinnacle of development before the motor industry and motorsport were halted by hostilities. With production and development halted, it is no surprise that the 328 came over a period to be perceived as highly desirable. It had the good fortune not to have its star eclipsed by the products of another manufacturer within a short space of time, which is the natural order of things in a competitive industry.

After the war ended, it was still to be some years before the industry was to regain the freedom and materials necessary to develop new models. It was the early 1950s before the first new postwar models from European manufacturers emerged, and when they did, they showed considerable progress from the 328. The Jaguar XK120, introduced in 1949, Lancia Aurelia in 1951, Alfa 1900 and 6C, each in their own way marked major steps forward.

None of these observations is meant to deny the 328 its place in automotive history. Instead they are an attempt to suggest the peculiar circumstances that have combined to give it the reputation it carries. Commercially the 328 was produced in numbers too small to be of great significance to the company. BMW devoted some effort to developing alloy-bodied streamlined versions for competition, and these models have widely

been seen as prototype replacements for the 328 that would have been introduced had war not intervened. The 328's competition success played a part in establishing the sporting credentials of the marque, and the model has been used in later years by the company to reinforce the aura of a long-established sporting pedigree.

The 328's reputation has grown with time as that of other marques has faded. BMW's success stems from the company's skill and vision in building a brand and inventing a tradition.

BMW's most significant early model, in terms of output, was of course the 326. It sold well and was in direct competition with the smallest of the Mercedes range. In late 1937, BMW sought to capitalize on a growing market for sporting cars by introducing the 327. Marketed as a sportier alternative to the 326, it was an elegant creation that is particularly appealing to modern eyes. Both as a closed coupe and as a cabriolet, it seemed particularly well proportioned, though interior room was sacrificed to style. Once again it was constructed from familiar components drawn from the existing product range. It combined the 310 chassis and front suspension with the rear suspension from the 328. Initially it was offered only with the 326 twin-carb engine, but from April 1938 could be had with the 328 alloy-headed three-carb unit, in which guise it was designated the 327/28.

FRANZ-JOSEF POPP

Franz-Josef Popp guided BMW through the interwar years. Originally an electrical engineer with AEG, Popp became involved in military procurement for the Austrian government during World War I, developing an expertise in aviation. He encouraged Ferdinand Porsche to develop a V-12 aircraft engine at Austro-Daimler and became the Austrian government's nominee to monitor development while the engine was produced in Germany by Flugwerke Deutschland. He remained in Germany and became initially technical director, and later general director, of the company as it evolved into BMW during the difficult postwar years. Popp was also on the Daimler-Benz board in the 1920s and was adept in developing industrial and government contacts. He was to remain at the helm of BMW for over 20 years, although he fell somewhat out of favor in government circles in the later 1930s, when he was perceived as reluctant to meet the increasing demands of the military authorities. By 1942 his company's delays in engine production and his refusal to agree to production quotas led to his being branded a saboteur and dismissed. He died in 1954.

Postwar, the model appeared in slightly modified, and less elegant form, as the Bristol 400, but around 2,000 327 models were produced before production ceased in 1941. It was revived postwar after the Eisenach factory came under East German control. The Soviet-controlled Autovelo concern produced a mildly modified version of the 327 from 1948 to 1955, albeit in small numbers. Quite a few of these were exported in an attempt to earn foreign currency.

Even rarer is the 335. This final prewar BMW was a long-wheelbase version of the 326 with a large, lightly stressed 3.5-liter engine. It was carefully designed to keep production cost low by using existing components. Though much bigger and heavier than the 326, it shared many body panels with the existing model. As a consequence, Ambi-Budd, which made the sedan body, had only limited retooling costs, and assembly could be readily integrated into the existing 326 lines at Eisenach. The 335 project was delayed significantly due to the limited capacity of the Eisenach works, but it made its debut, courtesy of AFN, at the British motor show in Olympia in 1938. The company built 400 before war halted production. The 335 was further evidence of BMW's desire to make what in today's jargon would be called a value-added product. Increasingly the company sought to sustain itself away from competition with volume producers like the GM-owned Opel and to move alongside Mercedes in the marketplace.

The company may have identified this market niche in part as a response to developments in taxation that had begun some years earlier. After the German government provided tax concessions, vehicle manufacturers enjoyed dramatic and sustained growth, given the otherwise slow level of consumer spending. From mid-1933, firms could recover nearly 70 percent of the original purchase price of a new vehicle. By late 1934 the German government extended the scheme to cover vehicle purchases by farmers, businessmen, and professionals, such as lawyers and doctors.

The government's push for a "people's car" further helped BMW to target its market. When it became clear that none of the private sector manufacturers could possibly meet the government's volume and price requirements for the proposed car, the state supported developments at Wolfsburg, where the VW was to be produced. The state's involvement with that project made it sensible for BMW to pursue other sectors of the market.

BMW, along with Daimler-Benz and Horch, received government investment subsidies, partly as a result of armament work they undertook. These subsidies were

not awarded to the mass manufacturers, Ford and Opel, due to their U.S. connections at a time when Germany was becoming increasingly concerned about developing as a self-sufficient world power.

Hitler's motorization policy—*motoreiserung*—was not just his personal interest and concern but one of the key elements in the conscious attempt to generate *initialzundung*—the "first spark" to create recovery in a depressed economy. Given the country's initial slow adoption of mass motoring, the government believed that creation of a vibrant motor industry could energize other sectors of the economy. While historians continue to debate the relative roles of rearmament, armament-related infrastructure development, and motor industry development as economic catalysts in the 1930s, there is no doubt BMW benefited and developed on the back of them.

Of course BMW was not just responding to the domestic market and domestic conditions. It wanted to export as well, and the government encouraged it to do so at a time when foreign exchange earnings were seen as essential. Germany badly needed foreign currencies to allow import of material needed to sustain rearmament. By 1938 the German motor industry was the major export earner, after electrical goods and coal. Ironically the United Kingdom was reputed to be a major potential market for the new 335, though that was not to be. BMW would not make inroads into the British market for some years, and it would be in a very different political and economic climate.

The 327's interior shows BMW's obsession with white plastic controls. Gearboxes were by Hurth or ZF and were rather fragile. Apparently the Volvo Amazon gearbox makes an ideal replacement!

CHAPTER 2

POSTWAR
SURVIVAL AND
BUILDING
A NEW FUTURE

Previous page: The ruins of the original BMW car factory at Eisenach were in the Russian-occupied part of Germany when hostilities ended. Eisenach workers beat their former colleagues on the other side of the Iron Curtain into production with a car. By the end of 1945, Eisenach had produced 68 prewar-style BMW 321s. These were followed up by 327 coupes and cabriolets that would remain in production until 1955, along with the 340—shown here—which blended postwar American styling with 335 bodywork from the A-pillar rearward. The cars were initially sold as BMWs but were renamed EMWs ("E" for Eisenach) when BMW in Munich began to take steps to stop the Russians using its badge. After 1955, the Eisenach factory produced Wartburg two-stroke economy cars.

Postwar Germany may seem an unlikely venue for what has been called an industrial miracle. Within a decade of the end of the war, Germany was beginning to emerge as a serious industrial power with an increasingly prominent role in sophisticated engineering and electronics. German consumer products were making headway in export markets, with the Volkswagen leading the way. This economic transformation becomes less surprising when you realize what was happening close to Germany's borders.

Germans lost the war, but the countries that had combined forces to beat them were an uneasy alliance. The United States was stronger than ever and determined to assume world leadership, yet it felt increasingly threatened by Russia and was hostile to its alternative social system. Under Russia's influence, communism was rapidly extending throughout Eastern Europe. Today we might look back on the cold war and conclude that only one outcome was possible in the clash between capitalism and communism. Just after the war, Western nations had no such confidence.

Russia played a key part in the war and secured influence and territory. During the period of rapid postwar change, the United States and Russia were growing mutually hostile. And what remained of Germany would become a new hotbed for East-West tensions. The ideological divide took physical form in the Berlin Wall, but Berlin was just a symbol of a wider contest between the two social systems. To prove the superiority of its social system, the West could not allow the rebuilding of West Germany to fail. Its economy would be the most obvious showpiece of capitalism's achievements. Setting bad memories and competitive concerns aside, massive forces worked to ensure Germany's success.

The interior of the EMW 340 shows some American influence with the column gearshift. In the domestic market, the cars were reserved for doctors and other professionals—no ordinary citizen could afford one. Quality was said to be awful. They were still in use as police cars in East Berlin in the 1960s.

Still, BMW had a difficult road ahead. During the war, the company had grown massively, in part through the infusion of workers from prisons and concentration camps. BMW was heavily involved in producing engines and military transport and had a leading role in the development of new aircraft engine technologies, on which Nazi hopes rested. These developments included axial flow turbojets and pure rocket motors. To reestablish the company after the war, with the Allies occupying Munich, BMW management required political skills and connections.

As a company BMW had effectively ceased to operate, and had little option but to think about a future that was new. In the United States and the United Kingdom, manufacturers revived the vehicles they had produced in the past, reestablishing the business on familiar lines using existing machinery and existing plants. BMW had no such options. The early days were precarious. Much of the existing BMW plant, tooling, and equipment had been secured by the Russians. The Eisenach plant, where car production had been centered, was located in the Russian-held zone. The company's other plants were initially prime reparations targets because of BMW's role as a key supplier to the German war effort. Yet with the Russians on

The elegantly bulbous 501 was BMW's first postwar passenger car. It was introduced in 1951, although production didn't begin until 1952. Here it lines up in front of a new postwar housing development in Munich.

Germany's doorstep, the West sought to minimize social dislocation in the country. Political analysts agreed that the World War I peace settlements, with their emphasis upon reparations, had played a part in creating a social and political climate conducive to fascism. Thus, the Western Allies eased up on their reparations demands.

BMW had to distance itself from its immediate past and use its friends in the banking sector and elsewhere to try to reopen business opportunities. Prewar the company had relied upon its airplane engine work. Now these plants were destroyed and there was no immediate prospect of rebuilding a future in this line of business. Their car plants were in East Germany, resuming production of the prewar models—initially as BMWs and later as EMWs. Other elements of the company's prewar production had found their way to England as war reparations, soon to give rise to the Bristol 400.

Critics have described the company's decision to develop the 501 and 502 sedans, in such uncertain conditions, as brave or even perverse. More serious reflection suggests otherwise. The immediate postwar Germany was a society scarred by poverty and dislocation. That society may have needed cheap, efficient transportation, but unless a manufacturer could profit from providing it, it was only a need, not an opportunity. Rather than build cheap cars for people who couldn't afford them, BMW gambled on those sectors of society who still had wealth and disposable income.

Other considerations influenced the decision. Large luxury sedans require less investment in production facilities than a vehicle targeted at mass production and produced in high volumes. At a time of acute materials shortages and economic unpredictability, management regarded high-volume production with price-sensitive customers and low unit margins as an unattractive route. Moreover, BMW had few resources other than the expertise of its returning work force, and its inclination and experience before the war had been focused on higher-end cars.

As early as 1946, Deutsche Bank was already attempting to revive the carmaker and was mobilizing resources to allow the company to think about production, albeit on a very limited scale. Initially the company produced whatever products it could, including cooking utensils, bicycles (with aluminum frames using leftover wartime materials), and various other components. It even explored the possibility of developing a small car—an attractive 600-cc design

The six-cylinder model used the old 2.0-liter engine and had ponderous performance, but this 502 used Germany's first postwar V-8 engine.

The rear isn't the most flattering view. Pundits likened its styling to cherubic angels found in baroque architecture. Except for extra chrome, there was little to separate the 6 and V-8 cars visually, apart from a bigger rear window on the latter. A basic V-8, called BMW 2.6, was offered, using less ornamentation. This 1960 502 is owned by Jim Smith.

similar to the Fiat Topolino, but with the BMW hallmark kidney-shaped grille. Few photographs remain of the elusive prototype, but it was surprisingly attractive and well conceived, combining small proportions with elegance and style in a way that few other small vehicles achieved. Yet for the reasons discussed above, BMW had no reason to challenge the formidable VW Beetle in the high-volume, low-cost market. Instead management chose to develop the 501 and 502 sedans—large, luxurious, high-performance sedans with a distinctive and attractive shape, to be powered eventually by a new alloy V-8 engine of modern design.

The big 501 sedan appeared first, in 1952, initially with an upgraded prewar six, which would run alongside the V-8s until 1958, with a total 9,973 units produced.

The car was underpowered, but it got the production lines moving—slowly; it took the company nearly a year after announcement to get the first batch to customers. The 501's styling received mixed reviews. Some found the look appealing, but critics argued that the bulbous shape and swirling lines carried only the worst features of Americanized styling, without the purity of design some U.S. models captured. Occasionally, as if to deride them further, they are compared to the Austin sedans of the immediate postwar era—the Devon, Somerset, and Hampshire. The slightly complex midmounted gearbox allowed a flat floor area, which, when combined with the column-mounted shifter, allowed room for five passengers and the driver. Initially the four-door bodies were hand-built by Baur, but with the assistance of Marshall Plan aid, BMW acquired body presses and tooling.

The interior still had a rather austere prewar flavor, but it was roomy and beautifully finished. Later cars have round instruments.

The all-alloy V-8 engine produced a modest 100 horsepower in its initial 2.6-liter form, giving a respectable top speed of 100 miles per hour in the hefty 502. It is rumored to have been the inspiration for the Buick Special engine of the early 1960s, which later became the famous Rover V-8.

When the rebuilding of the Milbertshofen plant was completed by 1954, the company began making bodies in greater numbers.

These big V-8 versions of the sedans, initially with a 2.6 V-8 and later with a 3.2-liter version, perhaps deserve more attention than they have received. Though conventional in terms of chassis layout, they had a better-located rear axle than contemporary Jaguars. Most important of all, they incorporated an advanced all-alloy V-8. Little attention has been paid to this engine, but it was the first postwar European V-8, and the wet liner all-alloy construction was ahead of its time. Contemporary commentators were impressed with its smoothness and torque spread. It certainly had significant development potential, producing reasonable power outputs with a tiny single carb and low compression. In service it proved powerful and trouble-free, and the 503 (later redesignated the 2600 and 3200) remained in service until 1963. The engine was reputedly not quite so successful in the 507, where examples imported to the United States were reportedly prone to overheating.

These sedans—and the 501 and its subsequent V-8 derivatives—never sold in large quantities, but BMW turned out a total of 21,000 of them in its 10-year production run. They reestablished BMW as a serious carmaker, while providing the basis for the much flashier 503 and 507 models. These two, like the 328 before them, captured the minds of enthusiasts even though they were produced in only nominal numbers. A mere 250 507s appeared, selling in the United

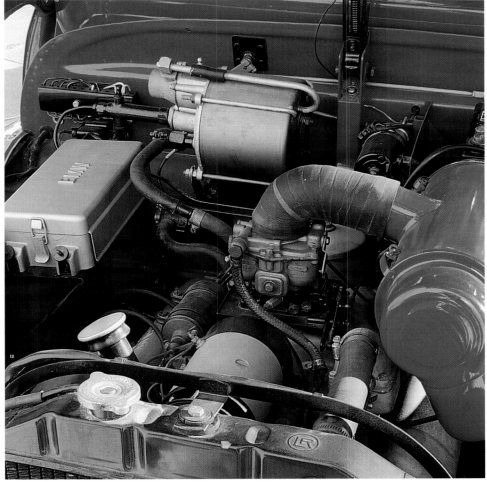

This shot shows the 502's rear-hinged "suicide" rear doors, another prewar affectation, which allowed easy access to the rear seats. With both doors open there was no central pillar. This method of construction was outlawed in Germany in the 1960s because it was found to be unsafe in a side-on collision.

States for nearly $9,000, yet they are the cars that are remembered by BMW aficionados—not that the majority will ever see one. Most authorities suggest that it was BMW's intention that a much larger number were to be made and that prices were to be much lower, but the hand-built nature of the car's construction made this impossible.

Much of the 507's fame lies in its rarity and the rather exaggerated claims made for it. The claimed top speed of 135-plus miles per hour, always qualified by the statement about this requiring the highest axle ratio available, must be evaluated in light of the stretch of straight road it would take to achieve it. With a curb weight of 2,935 pounds, despite it rakish light alloy body, this was no lightweight. Given a power rating of 150 to 160 horsepower (depending upon whom you believe), it is unlikely that the 507 could pull a usable final drive ratio allowing much more than 110 to 115 miles per hour. Of course, this was an era when manufacturers massaged performance figures upward without challenge from a compliant and enthusiastic motoring press—did any production line E-Type Jaguar ever achieve the 150 miles per hour of the heavily tuned press demonstrator?

Count Albrecht Goertz had worked for Studebaker in the United States and was allegedly encouraged by U.S. importer and entrepreneur Max Hoffman to design a car that would bring European style to a sophisticated segment of the U.S. market. Goertz had a background in industrial design and no one could question the beauty of the shape he produced for the 507. Correct in every detail, it was self-consciously stylish. Of course, other manufacturers of the period produced sports cars with real grace and sensuality. The original Austin Healey 100, despite its designer's relative anonymity, has a comparable aggressive stance, combined with correct proportioning. The Jaguar XK120 is a similarly graceful product. Aesthetically less successful was Mercedes' contender for sports car glory, the 300SL, while lesser marques, such as Triumph with the TR2 and MG with the TF and MGA, also failed to capture

As the badge shows, a bigger 3.2-liter version joined the 2.6 V-8 in 1955, pushing the top speed up to 105 miles per hour on 120 horsepower. The last of the V-8 sedan line was the 1961–1963 3200S, with a 160-horsepower engine. It was the fastest German production sedan of its day, with a top speed of 118 miles per hour. This car has been owned by Jim Smith since 1962.

The 507 was BMW's most dramatic flagship model since the 328, though it was more of a profile-raiser than a true production car—only 253 were built. Using the fairly pedestrian 502 chassis in shortened form, BMW clothed it in a roadster body of outstanding purity.

Front view shows how tall the 507 stands on its narrow center-knock steel wheels. The split shark-nose grille is a styling theme repeated on the latest Z8. The 507's body was built in aluminum.

that perfect suggestion of grace and power. Their cars were attractive and distinctive, but could not bear scrutiny for perfection from every angle in the way that the BMW can. The 507 also offered civilized creature comforts. It was a roadster in a sense that many of the other products weren't, having sedan-like ride and sophisticated interior appointments.

Whatever significance cars like the 502 and 507 had in maintaining BMW as a serious prestige automaker during the 1950s, they did not find enormous commercial success.

Neither did they capture the changes in the German market. Many writers on the company believe that BMW lost its way during this period. It's a difficult judgment to make with certainty. On the one hand BMW certainly did not challenge Mercedes in terms of volume manufacture of high-margin vehicles, nor did it

produce vehicles with the volume of small car manufacturers like Volkswagen, upon whom the reputation for quality engineering in the German auto industry was increasingly resting. By the mid-1950s, BMW adopted some typically pragmatic shortcuts. Purchasing the rights to build the Italian ISO-designed Isetta, but using BMW's established motorcycle–engine building capabilities, made commercial logic. At that point the market for small cars seemed buoyant and this purchase gave BMW immediate entry into a segment of the market that had caught popular imagination.

No longer were small cars of the "bubble car" variety seen as inferior products. Instead they were seen—at least until they were put to regular use—as distinctively modern. The company sought to distance the Isetta from poverty and economy and to relocate it into a world of style, fun, and convenience. They offered the

From the rear, you can appreciate the long hood, short rear deck proportions that give the shape its poise. The design was drawn by the industrial designer Count Albrecht Goertz at the behest of BMW's American importer Max Hoffman.

COUPE ELEGANCE—THE FORGOTTEN 503

Of the two glamorous new BMWs revealed at the Frankfurt Motor Show in 1955, the 507 roadster is the one that still holds the attention of marque enthusiasts and historians. It remained the pride of designer Count Albrecht Goertz's portfolio until, years later, he produced the Datsun 240Z. The 507 made his reputation but it was the 503, a svelte four-seater coupe and convertible that shared the stand that year, which more accurately predicted BMW's future. The closed version was the template for a dynasty of classic CS coupes that came to define the marque at its most glamorous. Students of automotive design have deified the 507 although, at the time, Battista Pinin Farina, one of the greatest car designers, preferred the 503 to the 507. Almost 50 years on, the shape still pleases, even if it is less obviously appealing than the 507.

If the 507 was meant to rival the 300SL, then the 503 was BMW's answer to the Mercedes 300S Coupe and Cabriolet, a large superluxury car with long-striding performance and superb build quality.

The overall proportions were exquisite, but the nose was a touch heavy-handed, with an exaggerated prow in the center and headlights that loom forward slightly too far. Goertz wanted them lower, but their height was preset by German rules. From a rear three-quarter angle, the thin pillars and the taper of the tail look perfectly judged.

The 507's glamorous roadster philosophy proved less durable as a marketable commodity. Only the current Z8 really draws on its heritage.

The driving force behind the 503 was Max Hoffman, whose distribution empire helped introduce Americans to the best European marques of the 1950s and 1960s, and the introduction of the Mercedes 300SL. Hoffman saw the need for a similar profile-raiser for BMW but at a lower price, to fill the gap between the gullwing and the cheap and cheerful MG TD. In other words, a modern interpretation of the 328.

Unimpressed by BMW's initial ideas for the car, Hoffman pointed the company in the direction of the 40-year-old Goertz, a

Raymond Loewy disciple who had risen from the position of airplane engine assembly-line worker before the war. Within a few months, BMW had committed itself to building two models, the 503 and 507, and Goertz had been hired to design them both. Neither car would be cheap enough to occupy Hoffman's suggested below 5,000 niche, but they were pitched squarely at the United States.

Before starting work on the 503, Goertz designed the gorgeous Starliner and Starlight coupes for Studebaker, and some similarities in line and proportion carried over to the BMW.

The quality of the aluminum body, hand-beaten by Graf Goertz (no relation) was superb. Panel gaps were slender and accurate, and the two huge doors closed with a stout but gentle "ker-plonk." It was a big car, its 15-foot, 6-inch overall length nearly as much as a modern 7 series.

Light, airy, and colorful inside with a commanding driving position and sumptuous seats, the 503 made a wonderfully opulent long-distance car. Space in the back wasn't generous, especially for your head, but the pillarless side window design was beautifully contrived. Front and rear windows withdrew electrically, and the front quarterlights had screw-operated catches. There was even the option of an electrohydraulic sunroof on the coupe.

Mechanically, the V-8 engine was the best part of the 503. This 90-degree pushrod unit had its block, heads, intake manifold, sump, timing cover, and clutch bell housing cast in aluminum, the pistons running in cast-iron wet cylinder liners. It was one of only three V-8s used in European cars at the time—the others were found in the French Ford Vedette (really a prewar side-valve Ford design) and the Czechoslovakian Tatra 603. For the 503—and 507—it was enlarged to 3,168 cc, the slightly lower state of tune used for the 503 giving 140 horsepower at 4,800 rpm. Compared with the smaller version, fueling was by two Zenith carburetors instead of one, compression ratio rose from 7.0:1 to 7.5:1, and an improved lubrication system provided the greater oil flow needed for the extra power.

Smooth and vibration-free, it combined low-down torque for minimal gear changing with the ability to rev freely to 5,750 rpm. The 3,307 pounds quoted by BMW was heavier than any Baroque Angel sedan—but the 503 could whisk up to cruising speeds that would have been well beyond the experience of most motorists in the 1950s. Zero to 60 could be run in around 13 seconds, the equal of an XK120 Jaguar, so the 503 didn't hang around. Early 503s—built before September 1957—had a column shift to go with

their layout, using a separately mounted gearbox positioned under the front seats. As a driver's car it mixed predictable, pleasant handling with a luxurious ride to make a consummate grand touring car. BMW's steering arrangement of the time is unique. The pinion on the end of the column meshes inside half a crown wheel, giving a sort of rack-and-pinion system, with the rack forming a semicircle. Beautiful and rare, the 503 ran from 1956 to 1959 and found 413 buyers, all of them in left-hand-drive markets.

Press shot of the 503 coupe, the Goertz-designed sister model to the 507 launched at the Frankfurt show in 1956. Running through to 1959, it too was a very low production model (410 built) using a lower powered 140-horsepower V-8.

A plush interior shows that BMW saw the 507 as more of a sports tourer than a proper sports car—it certainly never had the edge of aggression that made the 300SL Mercedes such an exciting car.

The 3.2-liter V-8 engine was the familiar unit from the 502, but now producing 150 horsepower. To give the handling some extra bite, a front anti-roll bar was fitted, but the 507 was never an especially nimble car. Top speed depended on the axle ratio—BMW claimed anything up to 136 miles per hour.

cars in bright colors. In its own way, the BMW-engined Isetta was a reasonably usable vehicle of its type. A large number were made and their popularity was enhanced by the sudden fuel scare caused by the Suez crisis of 1956. The Isetta also owed its success to a downturn in motorcycle demand. The prewar popularity of motorcycling as a means of transportation declined in Germany and elsewhere as living standards increased. Over 160,000 Isettas were made between 1955 and 1962, but profit margins were low. They were a fad that came and went, with few examples surviving in running order into the 1970s.

A larger and rather more attractive 600 model was produced between 1957 and 1959, which also sold quite well. The twin-cylinder 600-cc engine was more robust, allowing the vehicle to hold its own in traffic. The bodyshell offered something more closely approaching comfort, with a row of rear seats accessed by a side door to complement the original front opening. Around 35,000 were produced, enjoying a longer life than their smaller cousins. They remained a regular sight in German cities into the 1970s. Some even found their way south to Turkey and Greece, to give further service with returning migrant workers.

Commentators continually refer to the fact that the 600 introduced the semi-trailing arm rear suspension that was to become a feature of BMWs subsequently. It is difficult to be certain, but this arrangement probably

The Isetta "bubble car" was a successful attempt by BMW to get into the high-volume market with a cheap baby car. The design came from Iso in Italy. BMW produced the Isetta under a license agreement.

The Isetta was a rational solution to the problems of cheap urban transportation in the 1950s and despite its downmarket connotations seems to have done little to tarnish the firm's image.

This car is a United Kingdom-built three-wheeler Isetta. In the United Kingdom tricycles paid less road tax than four-wheeled vehicles. It has the later-type body style and is actually one of the last built in 1962. It was used by a member of Parliament as city transport.

appealed to the designers of the 600 because of the way it fed all stresses forward into a simple cross-member on the chassis, and was therefore simpler to make with the rear-engined layout than any other arrangement. The company placed more weight on the semi-trailing arm's impact upon chassis and body design and manufacture than on its efficiency as a suspension.

By 1959 the 600 was beginning to look old-fashioned and was facing competition from cars by NSU and Renault that had more aesthetic appeal. Small cars in general were about to be challenged decisively by the Mini, while Ford, Triumph, and DKW were about to introduce new models that they and competitors knew were to be major improvements over their predecessors. Small car design had moved forward, and BMW placed its hopes in a new monocoque sedan and coupe series it designated the 700. Once again, the model featured a twin-cylinder motorcycle-derived engine, but this time clothed in an attractive Michelotti-designed body.

The 700 range was a well-engineered package, attractive in appearance and with sufficient performance to make them fun to drive. The coupes attracted attention in racing—though they never had the outright performance potential of the Mini—and were generally well received. In various guises, the company produced

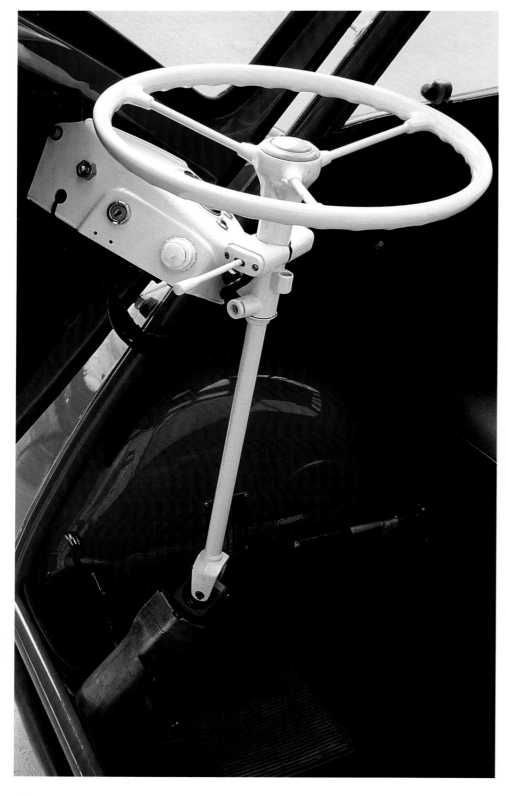

This shot shows the way the Isetta's front door was actually the whole of the front of the car, bringing the steering column with it when the door was opened.

nearly 200,000 examples, and while profit margins were not large, this level of sales played their part in keeping BMW afloat during one of its most troubled periods. As a model, the 700 perhaps appeals more in retrospect than in the metal. It was, after all, a very small car styled with the proportions of a larger car. The result was attractive to look at but not particularly spacious to ride in. Seat cushions were wafer thin, wheel arches intrusive, and door panels flat and resonant. Simplicity at times gave way to starkness. Though build quality was reasonable and they were agile in traffic, they remained noisy and tiring for long journeys.

During the early 1960s the BMW product range ran from the small 700 economy cars in sedan and coupe variants to the large, V-8–engined 2600 and 3200 sedans, which were perhaps now beginning to appear a little aged, although they remained capable vehicles. The company also continued to produce the Isetta until 1962, in three- or four-wheel configuration to suit different countries' licensing and taxation regulations. At the other extreme, BMW introduced

The minimalist Isetta dashboard bore only a speedometer and a few warning lights. Drivers changed gear with in the left hand. Top speed was a respectable 53 miles per hour using a single-cylinder BMW motorcycle engine.

THE BMW-BRISTOL CONNECTION

At the end of the 1939–1945 war, the Bristol Aeroplane Company found itself with spare production capacity. The directors believed there was a market for a sporting sedan built to aircraft standards. Enter Lt. Col. H.J. Adlington, of AFN, who had marketed the prewar BMWs in Britain under the BMW-Frazer-Nash brand with some success. He heard of Bristol's car-making ambitions through his brother Don, who worked at the Ministry of Aircraft Production and was posted at the Bristol works at Filton. H.J demonstrated a prewar 327/80 to the Bristol directors, and before long a Stirling bomber, loaded with BMW drawings and parts acquired as "war reparations," was on its way to Filton. BMW engineer Fritz Fieldler was released from prison—where he, like Dr. Porsche, was being held as a "war criminal"—and he was seconded to help develop the new Bristol car, which was to be based on the 327 coupe. The car was announced to the press as the Frazer-Nash Bristol in September 1946, although differences in philosophies meant that the two concerns would soon part company.

As a result of the split, which Adlington did not to oppose, Dr. Fielder moved to Frazer-Nash, where he penned the postwar Frazer-Nash—reputedly in one month of concentrated design and drawing activity. Adlington also secured an agreement allowing his independent concern to purchase BMW-derived Bristol engines at a favorable rate while conceding that the new car would emerge under the Bristol name. The close-coupled 400 coupe was steel-bodied with a wooden body frame. It used the sophisticated 328 engine in a torsion bar–suspended, rack-and-pinion-steered chassis, which was largely that of the prewar BMW. The car was good for 95 miles per hour and was twice the price of a contemporary Jaguar, reflecting not just the purchase tax on luxury goods during the austere postwar period but also the undoubted high quality of the car. Four hundred seventy-one 400s were built up to 1948, when the 401 was announced with a more modern aerodynamic style—now wrought in alloy—that took its inspiration from Italian-bodied touring prototypes that appeared earlier in the same year. The 400 series Bristols would get progressively heavier and more luxurious as the 1950s progressed, culminating in the 1958 406, with its disc brakes and slightly more powerful 2.2-liter engine.

The company was beginning to recognize the need for a more powerful engine. When the car manufacturing side of the firm was split from aircraft manufacturing (to become part of BAC—the British Aircraft Corporation) the straight six was finally abandoned in favor of a 4.7-liter Chrysler V-8. Chrysler-engined Bristols are still made to this day, but the chassis, with the same 9-foot, 6-inch wheelbase, is recognizably related to the 1946 400 and, thus, the prewar BMWs.

the 3200CS coupe in 1962 with Bertone-designed four-seater body and V-8 engine.

BMW had a curiously varied product range during this period. In terms of establishing a brand image, that may often be counterproductive, but BMW's position may not have been so irrational as is often supposed. The company was in a perilous financial state for much of the period, yet whether that was a product of the diversity of its range is by no means certain. Despite its problems, BMW did survive when quite a lot of the German motor industry did not. Auto Union, DKW, Borgward, and Hansa all experienced periods of difficulty. NSU, Goggomobil and Glas similarly struggled, and eventually succumbed.

BMW's wide range of vehicles actually cost it relatively little to develop and build. The Isetta was an outside design acquired to catch a perceived market opportunity. Its development was cheap, utilizing existing motorcycle running gear. Similarly the 700 range used tried and tested components and required limited investment in its development and production. The sedan and coupe shared mechanicals and much of their panelwork. These were vehicles produced with a keen eye on costs and returns.

The 600 was a four-seater alternative to the Isetta introduced in 1957 and was a step toward a "real" car, although it still looked rather like an Isetta and retained the front door arrangements.

The large sedans brought the marque prestige, and development costs were spread over a long period. Of course the 503 and 507 models were expensive to build, and could seem an unjustifiable indulgence for a company in BMW's position, yet they had a disproportionate effect on the image of the marque. Produced in very small numbers, and effectively hand-built, one wonders whether BMW really did ever believe they would be large sellers. Perhaps the company made a conscious decision that even though they could not be sold in large numbers they would have a positive effect on perception

of the marque. At a time when Mercedes-Benz was once again capturing attention in world motoring circles with its Grand Prix and Sports Racing 300SLR, as well as the charismatic 300SL, BMW perhaps needed the 503 and 507 to maintain its image. After all, the Isetta hardly placed BMW at the prestigious end of the motoring spectrum.

Whatever can be said about BMW's model range at this time, the company, along with the rest of the German motor industry, was undergoing significant change in the later 1950s. On the one hand, Germany

The 600 was a grown-up four-seater Isetta with one side door and Isetta-like front opening door, but powered by a two-cylinder BMW motorcycle engine. The company turned out 34,813 examples from 1957 to 1959.

The 600 was powered by a twin-cylinder 582-cc engine seen here, and could manage 62 miles per hour flat out. It was the first BMW to feature semi-trailing arm rear suspension, an arrangement the company remained faithful to until the 1990s.

had dramatically transformed its fortunes. It was now seen as a leader in engineering and technology and making rapid inroads into consumer markets world-wide. Within West Germany itself, some portion of the benefits were trickling down to all levels within the society. The social market economy was working, and the virtuous cycle of high investment and high productivity led to a situation in which German exports increased dramatically. Yet alongside this there is evidence of significant rationalization and concentration within the industry.

For BMW in the 1950s, turnover increased year after year with a pleasing upward trend. On the other hand, profitability remained more problematic. BMW had alternated between profit and loss for most of the years between reformation in 1946 and 1955. By the mid-1950s the motorcycle market, on which it had become quite dependent, began to contract. At the same time the company's financial management seemed less assured. The attempts to regain a footing in the airplane engine business proved initially very costly, and losses mounted. There was also an ideological schism within German politics and industry. Public policy and political sentiment lauded competition. But industrialists and bankers wanted stable and controlled conditions

with high profitability. Rapid concentration, and controlled competition, were the order of the day.

Clearly BMW, as a cash-strapped producer, was an unlikely bet for the major investment required to fund development of new models—even though the benefits of doing so were evident. Help came, indirectly, through government action at the regional level. The Bavarian regional government in 1959—at the height of the crisis—offered BMW loans conditioned on the resignation of Finance Director Dr. Richter Brohm. The banks also sought the restructuring of the company, proposing a new share issue to be held by them and Daimler-Benz AG. A meeting of small shareholders challenged the banks' proposals and the company rejected the restructuring.

Uppermost in the shareholders minds was likely the fact that the proposals involved writing down by half the value of their shareholdings. Fortunately their activity awakened the interest of others who could see opportunity and potential. The wealthy Quandt family became involved and over a period gained a controlling stake in the company. In some ways, these dominant private figures would move the company away, perhaps for the first time, from the mainstream of the German industrial model. Industrial ownership in Germany did not, and does not, normally feature dominant and distinctive individuals as owners. BMW was to build upon its past, but also break with it, in its new phase of development.

The 3200CS completes the story of BMW's postwar V-8s, but in style is really a link with the next generation of big coupes. The shape by Bertone of Italy looked not unlike the contemporary Gordon Keeble and Alfa 2600 Sprint Coupes. Under the skin was the old cocktail of 1951 chassis and late-1950s 3.2-liter V-8 engine in 160-horsepower tune. The bodywork was shipped from Italy to be mated with the chassis.

This one-off convertible 3200CS was built for a director of BMW and was considered for production. In total 603 fixed-head 3200CS models were built.

CHAPTER 3

THE 1960s:
THE *NEU CLASSE* SEDAN AND THE PHENOMENON OF THE 2002

Previous page: The 1965–1969 2000 coupe was an interesting flagship model based on the *neu classe* but with a two-door pillarless body by Karmann. It was styled in-house at BMW but was heavily influenced by the previous 3200CS. The four-headlight arrangement was for the United Kingdom market only.

The interiors of the coupes were luxurious with lots of hand-finished wood and opulent seats. They were rather heavy compared to the sedans, however, so performance suffered a little.

The conventional wisdom, naturally appealing to the enthusiast, is that BMW's inspired decision to produce a new range of quality midrange sporting sedans was rewarded with commercial success. The argument is that the products were so good that the company triumphed on the basis of customer choice. Such an interpretation chimes in well with the image of a free market economy, in which consumer sovereignty brings rewards to the most innovative and productive producers. It can be supported by favorable press comment on the new cars and there is no difficulty in finding evidence that the new BMW 1500 sedan, and especially the later 1800, 2000, and 2002 models, were appreciated by car buyers both at home and abroad. Perhaps it is an interpretation that is too neat to be wholly convincing.

The production of a midsize sporting sedan had been one of BMW's objectives from the late 1950s. Recruits to BMW from that period recall often hearing about the project without much evident sign of progress toward development or production. Funds were limited and the necessary finance seemed uncertain. It was not until the Frankfurt Show of 1961 that the new model was finally to appear, and even then only in prototype form. Some months of further development were required before customers would receive their new cars. Compared to the midrange Ford and General Motors products offered in Germany at that time, it represented

a major advance. It was not that the new model contained any particular technical novelty, nor was initial build quality so high that the early cars did not have their problems. Rather it was the elegance with which the whole package was constructed that marked it out from its competitors. Restrained styling was combined with excellent handling and a bright modern appearance.

It was, of course, very well received and certainly in Germany there was a sense that BMW had produced a vehicle that was both practical transport and an aspirational product for the future. Its style and functionality

suited an age when Germany had finally emerged from the aftermath of war and once again become a confident nation. The car's appearance and construction expressed engineering values rather than fashion or style gimmickry. In this way it was in tune with the attitudes and values of an age when technological progress seemed to offer real options for the future—an age where rationality and scientific appraisal were taking the place of convention, tradition, and received wisdom. With its new range, BMW was addressing a new, modern, confident postwar Germany.

The 1960s, compared to earlier years, was a period when the affluent marked themselves off from the crowd less by flamboyant display than by increasingly subtle differences. BMW was embarking on the road of making classy rather than flamboyant cars. The affluent public's shift from flashy to classy was occurring to an extent all across Europe—a change BMW would both shape and benefit from with its new line of cars.

Postwar Europe retained its social divisions while inequalities of wealth and income remained large. Nevertheless, the cultural conventions about the display of

The new class (*neu classe*) marked BMW's return to prosperity in the 1960s. Here an 1800 saloon lines up with the hand-finished, Karmann-built 2000CS coupe

The final version of the *neu classe* was the 2000 saloon, identifiable by its oblong headlights and new horizontal taillights. It was available with manual or BMW's first automatic transmission, built by ZF. There were twin-carburetor and Kugelfischer fuel injection versions also. The car lived on until the introduction of the 5 series in 1972.

BMW 2000

BMW 2000 C Automatic

wealth were changing. Accident of birth or inherited wealth seemed less acceptable as justification for inequality in the 1960s. Not that inequality itself was rejected. On the contrary, affluence came increasingly to be interpreted by both the fortunate, and the wider society, as a legitimate reward for educational attainment or technical competence. Whereas those of a previous generation could express their social position through their inherited tastes, manners, rituals, and connections, a new generation needed new social markers. Possessions lost none of their power to express social position, but the criteria for their selection changed. Function and performance were the seemingly neutral criteria that the affluent came to see as guiding their choices. Rationality, rather than indulgence, was to be the preferred hallmark of the new elite of managers, professionals, and technocrats who were to form the BMW customer base

BMW, for example, has since the 1960s produced a top-of-the-range model that shares the bulk of its styling features with its smaller cousins. From

the outset, commentators remarked upon the simple unadorned exterior of the 1500 sedan as well as its functional interior and dashboard. The notion of upmarket and expensive vehicles being discreet, familiar, yet somehow different and appealing, was increasingly being recognized as the key to the future.

The public's interest in new displays of wealth, including classy automobiles, affected young people too, making them much more vehicle literate than any previous generation. Cars were accepted and no longer novel. A specialist media had grown up—subservient to the manufacturers yet instrumental to some extent in developing new criteria by which vehicles were to be judged. The "new class" BMW fit in well with these trends.

The features of the *neu classe* are well known. At their base was a sturdy, four-door monocoque shell with large bonnet and boot panels extending the full width of the car and forming a pronounced waistline. The suspension, with MacPherson struts up front and semi-trailing arms at the rear, allowed large, well-controlled suspension movement,

and it was cheap to produce. The overall design provided good ride quality and gave passengers excellent insulation from noise and harshness.

Trim and fittings were simple, elegant, and made of good quality materials. It may be that much of the German car manufacturers' growing reputation for quality can be attributed to their ability to motivate and coordinate their suppliers. Minor fittings, electrical components, trim, seals, and fasteners all seem both simpler and more integrated with the vehicle design on German-manufactured vehicles of this period compared to products from other countries. Suppliers and manufacturers elsewhere seemed as often in conflict, both financially

and in an engineering sense, as in harmony. The new engine was in no way revolutionary, but a nice modern design with a single chain-driven overhead cam in an alloy head. It was a unit designed with large margins of strength and safety, allowing for increased capacity as necessary. The company initially produced examples with an alloy block but a more conventional iron block was found in production models.

The press has always given the *neu classe* very positive treatment. As time has passed, however, and BMW's reputation has grown, perhaps hindsight has tended to encourage us to overlook what certain other manufacturers were doing. It is too easy to compare the

The 02 series was a huge success for BMW, and really established its name in the North American market. Here was a compact car that mixed quality with driver appeal and reasonable running costs—it was everything the domestic American car wasn't.

new BMW with the rather uninspired existing midrange sedans from the European operations of Ford and General Motors. The Ford Consul and Taunus, Opel Rekord, and Hillman Minx in their various guises were rooted in the 1950s in both engineering and image. Against them, the BMW looks in a different league.

For a fairer comparison one might look elsewhere. BMW's new offerings were not unique. In Italy, Alfa offered the new agile Giulia, which could easily make the BMW look cumbersome. Fiat introduced the more mundane 1500 sedan, but it still proved a vigorous performer. Lancia offered the new Flavia which, as always with Lancias, seemed better than the sum of its parts. In

the United Kingdom many midrange models remained dreary, combining awful build quality with miserable road behavior. With the advent of the Cortina though, new standards were being set. The days of the cumbersome Oxfords and Minxes with their crudely designed bodyshells, random substructure of rust-trapping box sections, and massive front cross-members were numbered. While it may seem sacrilege to compare the Cortina to the BMW, the Cortina introduced new engineering approaches to bodyshell construction and production costing that had great influence in subsequent years. Designed for ease and cheapness of assembly, Ford produced a bodyshell that was both lighter and

The 1600-2 kicked the series off in 1966, but it was the 2002 that really captured buyers' imaginations. By slotting its biggest engine in its lightest body, BMW created a show room hot rod that looked entirely innocent.

stiffer than previous efforts. Ford engineers addressed the issue of ventilation properly for the first time: with its eyeball vents, a Cortina was a better place to be than many more expensive sedans, BMW 1500 included, on a hot muggy day.

Other companies with limited resources, such as Rover and Triumph, clearly set their sights on a similar market. Their respective 2000 models both catered to slightly different tastes, with the technically complex

Rover presenting a refined image compared to the simpler, and more brash, Triumph. Yet both cars were worthy competitors in design to the new BMWs, though both were poorly executed in production. Saddled with engines that did not inspire, both the Triumph and the Rover were still able to provide good performance and, by the standards of the day, responsive road behavior. Clearly by 1962 to 1963 BMW did not have the sort of obvious superiority over its competitors that

could account for the marque's reversal of fortunes. In fact, even the much-lauded concept of a large engine in a small body, which has come to be associated with the later BMW 2002, was anticipated in a primitive way by Triumph with its Vitesse.

Perhaps a better comparison for gauging BMW's success during this period comes from other long-established German carmakers—Borgward and Glas. From the mid-1950s Borgward had produced the fine Isabella

sedan, which combined technical innovation with modern styling. The car came in a variety of forms: a large two-door sedan, stylish coupe, and one of the first wagons that was not a mere design afterthought but a properly engineered model. The Isabella was technically innovative and developed a strong following of satisfied customers. The Bremen-based company was one of three car producers under the personal ownership of Dr. Carl Borgward, a rather autocratic and individualistic character with aristocratic values and attitudes.

During the height of BMW's troubles, he had considered the BMW factories (along with numerous other manufacturers) as a possible means for expanding production of the Isabella, possibly under the name BMW Isabella. By 1961 Borgward held about 5 percent of the domestic market and its models were successfully exported around the world. At this point it had a larger market share than BMW and had products of proven quality along with a newly introduced, large Big Six sedan. The firm employed nearly a quarter of the Bremen work force and was regarded as a center of technical excellence.

Nevertheless, with a cyclic downturn in 1961, Borgward met a cash flow crisis that the banks were unwilling to resolve. The Bremen state government intervened, as the Bavarian state government did with BMW, but the

This later-American-market 2002 shows the big bumpers demanded by federal rules, and square taillights— collectors tend to prefer the round taillights of the earlier cars. The "Tii" badging denotes fuel injection.

BMW bought the struggling Glas concern in 1966 for 91 million deutschmarks. This is one of the cars it inherited: the Frua-styled 1700GT coupe with belt-driven overhead camshaft engine. (Glas pioneered this.)

Glas, like Borgward, was a victim of BMW's success in the 1960s. BMW bought the firm merely to gain production capacity, and killed off the interesting Glas 1300/1700GT.

outcome was very different. After restructuring, with the removal of Dr. Borgward, the state government sought a buyer for the company without success. Appeals to the banks, other manufacturers and the federal government were rejected. It lapsed into liquidation with a significant adverse affect on the local economy.

On the one hand, this can be explained in terms of the economic situation Borgward was in and the relative financial weakness of the Bremen state government in comparison with their richer and more assertive Bavarian counterparts. On the other hand, it has been argued by historian Simon Reich and others that compared with the efforts that were made at every level to save BMW from liquidation or foreign ownership, Borgward

generated much less concern. Reich has speculated that the local political balance had a part to play. The Bremen state government was led by the SPD, while the federal government under Chancellor Erhard, had a Christian Democrat majority. The CDU may well have felt that the demise of Borgward would undermine the popularity of the SPD in Bremen and give the CDU advantage at the next state elections.

Whatever the short-term political issues that may have influenced the pattern of events, more deep-rooted issues need to be considered. One way that historians have tried to understand the evolution of the postwar German auto industry is to examine its relation to the state. This approach suggests that the corporatist

BMW gradually discontinued the various Glas models in order to expand production at the Dingolfing factory, but the 1700GT, along with the desirable 3000GT coupe, was given a brief stay of execution, becoming the BMW 1600 coupe with BMW semi-trailing arm rear suspension and twin-carb 1600 engine. It only lasted a year and the last ones were sold off at bargain prices.

Baur produced first a fully
open-topped convertible on
the 1600-2 chassis and then
this 2002 cabriolet with a
Targa roof panel. It's 110
pounds heavier than the
standard 2002 and not an
altogether happy thing to
look at.

doctrines that came to the fore during the fascist period were not aberrations, but marked an integral part of German industrial development. The postwar governments discarded the fascist policies but retained the corporatist instinct and used it to create economic success. Reich, for example, has argued that you can identify two separate groups of manufacturers: One group, in which BMW was located along with VW, Daimler-Benz, Porsche, and NSU-Audi, were manufacturers who historically had close connections with the state. The other group tended to have very much more strained state relations. They comprised the German offshoots of U.S. companies, Opel and Ford, which the German government always viewed as outsiders, along with Borgward, which, due to the character of the owner, had avoided close connections with the state and charted an independent course. Access to financing and extensive state support during difficulties tended to be offered more readily and effectively to those firms at the core of the government's vision of its industrial future. Those firms outside

the charmed circle either survived and prospered because of their connections with parent companies in the United States, or found themselves herded into the control of the core firms.

Borgward was simply abandoned to the market, and the company went into liquidation. Glas, a similarly inventive and successful small manufacturer, was quickly swallowed and obliterated by BMW, once it found itself in difficulty.

The Italian-styled Glas saloons and coupes were elegant and offered some technical novelty. They were the first cars to use toothed rubber belt drive for the camshaft. While they were well thought of, they never made money for the company, whose only profitable line was its Goggomobil economy cars.

Not only did the downfall of Borgward, and later Glas, rid the market of two potential competitors for BMW and its new range, but in each case it released a large number of excellent designers and engineers into the job market just when key technical labor shortages

were posing a problem for BMW and the rest of the industry. Key Borgward personnel found their way to BMW and played their part in developing the marque.

While this was taking place, a series of mergers and rationalizations, inspired by government, were serving to strengthen the "native" core of the German auto industry at the expense of the U.S. offshoots, Opel and Ford.

By 1963 the general shape of the German industry had emerged, and it was not until the advent of Japanese competition and the reawakening of Ford and Opel in the 1980s that the industry was to face threat once again. By that time, however, BMW was no longer a marginal player, with a weak product line-up and mounting debt, but a confident producer with a defined and profitable global market niche.

By 1963 BMW was paying shareholders a 6 percent dividend. Its production, though still modest, was profitable and the 1500 had spawned a larger and more sporting 1800 variant. Whatever the brochures and press handouts may have said, the 1500 always had to work quite hard to shift this quite large sedan at the sporting pace owners desired. An 1,800-cc version was a distinct improvement. Early in 1964, the hotter 1800Ti emerged, followed by a small number of 1800Ti/SA homologation specials designed primarily for competition work.

BMW had reopened a competition department and once again used motorsport as a way of promoting its image worldwide. Although it had significant success, its efforts were rather undermined by the dominance of Ford in competition. Lightweight Lotus Cortinas were significantly quicker than the BMWs, and BMW wisely sought to avoid head-to-head competition. The fast but fragile Cortinas could dominate in shorter races, but the BMWs did excel over longer distances. Of course what mattered in motorsport, then as now, is not the results themselves but the way they are represented, and BMW was as adept as Ford in linking its brand with the image of track success.

As the 1500 and 1800 were stealing the limelight and generating the profits, the older models had quietly been axed. The Isetta struggled on until 1962, while the big sedans were discontinued in 1963. The last of these, renamed the 3200S with more power and a wider rear window, was still a match for most of its rivals in terms of performance and presence, but sales remained low and the company's energies could more profitably be concentrated elsewhere. The 700 remained in production, as did the large 3200CS coupe.

While the product range was being rationalized, some restructuring was also taking place in the dealer

The interiors were upgraded on later 2002 cars with a "safety" padded steering wheel and token wood trim around the instruments.

The Touring estate version of the 02 was a good idea, but its frumpy styling failed to catch on. Launched in 1971, it was quietly dropped in 1974.

network. Much of this was linked to the appointment of an enigmatic new head of marketing, Paul Hahnemann. He would have an important influence on the way BMW was to develop. Hahnemann joined BMW from Auto Union, where he worked after learning his marketing skills at Opel.

Hahnemann brought U.S. marketing flair to BMW at a crucial time, along with a sensitivity to the cultural changes unfolding in Germany and elsewhere. BMW was moving up a gear, yet the marketing, service, and after-sales network had remained poorly organized and poorly motivated. More particularly, management wanted dealerships to project the new image of BMW and capture the kind of customers for which the new range had been designed. Dealers were put under pressure to perform, and

feted when they did. The company was represented in many areas by quite small workshops, and the advent of the desirable new range of cars gave an opportunity for these concerns to grow and develop.

Slowly BMW was coming to acknowledge openly that it was a company driven by marketing rather than engineering. Engineering values and technical competence

NEU CLASSE VERSUS ROVER 2000

In the early 1960s many pundits wouldn't have given good odds on BMW seeing out the decade. If you'd predicted BMW owning Rover 30 years later, those same pundits would split their drip-dried shirts laughing.

In 1963 BMW was a company that could only look over the water at Rover and dream, although there were certain parallels to be drawn. Both had worked on jet engine technology in the war and traded on a reputation for high-quality engineering. Both had built big cars in the 1950s largely for a home audience. Both recognized the need to diversify. In Rover's case, the savior was the Land Rover, and it was the money earned from this in foreign markets that developed the 2000, or P6.

The name BMW would have elicited quizzical looks from many people in Britain in 1963. It was an obscure marque with a sprinkling of dealerships and a certain prewar reputation, among those who could remember, created by a handful of highly priced sports cars. It didn't even have a proper concessionaire, but was sold through a dealership—AFN—and was probably best known for its Isetta bubble cars, which had largely been wiped from the collective memory by the Mini. Very few people were aware of its high-priced V-8 sedans and sports cars.

As we know, the blueprint for BMW chassis engineering was laid down with the 1500 saloon, but in many ways the Rover was a far more ambitious design. Its DeDion rear suspension ensured that it gripped the road like a sports car and rode like a limo. Its base unit construction—not unlike a Citroen DS—was a steel skeleton to which all the suspension and mechanics were attached. The body panels were unstressed, and the P6's base unit

was uncommonly strong in a crash. It was released to rave reviews in the autumn of 1963, not just because of its refinement and, at the time, astonishing road holding, but because it was one of the first British cars—perhaps the first British car—to address safety issues. It had proper four-wheel disc brakes (inboard at the back, where the BMW only ever had drums), a generously padded interior and that muscular base unit. Seat belts were standard in the 2000 two years before they became mandatory. Outwardly it was a slender, beautifully detailed car and easily one of the best-looking sedans of its generation. There's nothing trick or showy, which was why the car looked so fresh for so long. The BMW was boxier, more severe with harsh, angular lines—which originated in Italy—that didn't age quite so well although the tall, glassy greenhouse set the trend for later BMWs in its modernist simplicity. The shark nose and the kicked-up rear side window were themes BMW maintained but it seemed to sit high on its narrow little steel wheels, with an awkwardly high trunk lid that at least promised a massive trunk.

Whereas the BMW was austere and unremarkable inside—no more plush than a contemporary VW in some ways—the Rover with its shin bins, its ergonomically designed controls (a first in a British car), and its safety padding was one of the high points of 1960s interior design.

It's interesting to look back at contemporary reports on the cars. While the BMW had been received with polite interest as another rational, sporty German sedan, the magazines went wild for the 2000. *Car and Driver* said it was "Absolutely the best sedan that has ever been presented in these pages" and that if "every car on the road was as good as this one, they could raise the speed were a key part of the company image, but its course was determined by marketing opportunity and marketing perceptions. Of course this was this same mix of instincts that had guided the company through the prewar period. Even though it may have lost its way somewhat in the first postwar decade, there was still evidence that this was a company with a feel for the world around it.

Technical innovation and engineering excellence were means to an end, not an end in themselves.

By the early 1960s, top management required William Geishen, the ex-Borgward production chief who now managed BMW production, to seek final approval from marketing on a range of matters regarding the development of the car. The company began to address in a

limit in the country 15 miles per hour and still have a reduced accident rate." Even so, the great American public largely ignored the Rover, and Americans were never to buy the P6 in very large numbers. The 2002, a direct development of the 1500, would eventually sell in huge numbers in North America. Certainly the BMW, especially in its later injected or twin-carb form, would have been a less-compromised driver's car than the Rover. Certainly its engine had the edge in terms of smoothness and response—the Rover's unit always felt a bit harsh and unenthusiastic. And while ultimately it didn't ride or hold the road as well as the Rover, it rolled less and felt more "involving."

BMW was enjoying the resurgence it hoped the *neu classe* would give it. Racing success in the European Touring Car Championship raised the model's profile as the capacity increased first to 1,800 cc and then, in 1966, to 2.0 liters and 100 horsepower. In some markets the car got slinky, oblong headlights and a revised tail but in the United Kingdom, at least initially, it had compromised four-headlight styling on the single-carb model and, bizarrely, two headlights on the 2000Ti with its twin Solex carburetors and 120 horsepower. By this time a proper concessionaire had been set up in the United Kingdom to deal exclusively with the make. The former importer, AFN, was marketing a Frazer-Nash version of the Ti with special badges and a wooden gear knob and steering wheel.

In Britain the appreciation of continental cars generally, and BMWs in particular, was growing as the barrier of high duty began to fall. Middle class professionals liked the air of reserved sophistication and purposeful engineering that suffused these cars.

Yet Rover was still the brightest star in the executive car galaxy, a focal point of middle class aspirations in Britain. Rover's near-fatal merger with BMH in 1967 appeared seamless at the time, as the Solihull factory that had been created specially for the 2000 produced its 10,000th example. Somehow the P6 would never be tainted by the British Leyland debacle, although as it moved into its final chip-cutter grille phase in 1971 it began to hint, visually, at the dumbing-down of the marque's values from the mid-1970s onward. Inside, cloth began to take the place of leather and too many trim strips and cheap-looking badges began to deflower the purity of the original shape.

There was less and less money for development, as Rover's profits were tipped into the black hole that was British Leyland, and its products became the mass-market lame ducks—cars like the Allegro and Maxi—we know so well. As the P6 and the Rover spirit ebbed away under the tyranny of British Leyland, BMW boomed, riding the crest of aspirational popularity from which it has never really descended. The 2000 sedan, though it carried on until 1972, had long since been usurped by the 2002 and the new large, handsome six-cylinder 2500 3.0-liter cars. The 2000's effective replacement as BMW's middle-ranking saloon was the 5 series.

If the *neu classe* was the car that cast the modern mold for the BMWs of today, the P6 was really the last decent Rover. In its combination of quality, compactness, and upwardly mobile aspirations, it embodied everything that we came to hold dear, years later, in the BMW 5 series. Had Rover maintained its standards and built a modern P6, a 1970s interpretation, it could have taken BMW on at its own game, rather than being taken over by BMW, dismembered, and discarded.

Certainly the "ultimate" 2002 has to be the Turbo. It predicted a trend for forced induction that would take hold in the 1980s, although the car seemed ill-timed when it was introduced at the Frankfurt show in 1973—just as the oil crisis was beginning to take hold.

new, systematic fashion the way BMW was to be marketed, reflecting and shaping the public's perception of the marque.

The invention of traditions, in which a convenient imagined past is adapted to the needs of the day, had been the hallmark of nineteenth- and twentieth-century nationalisms. It was now to become part of the promotion of a consumer product. Mid-1960s BMW sedans were increasingly being photographed alongside some of their forbears—in particular the 328. Advertisements

spoke of a tradition of sporting achievement. Conscious efforts were made to associate the marque with innovation, activity, and achievement.

Implicit in much of this activity was an attempt to depict competitors' vehicles—particularly Mercedes—as fine for the complaisant and unadventurous but not appropriate for a new generation. Both Quandt and Hahnemann were much taken with the doctrine that the car's value must be expressed in its price. Reversing the logic of many sellers, they recognized that new, high-spending customers would be sensitive to the car's image and quality. The fact that the vehicles were expensive would simply be confirmation of their taste in distinctive and well-made cars. BMW, in fact, had little option on the price of the 1500 and 1800, as their initial price projections for the models had proved unrealistic. Originally promised at around 8,500 deutsch marks, they ended up well over 9,000 deutsch marks when they became available. Already almost 25 percent more expensive than the midrange cars available from mass manufacturers, BMW kept its faith in added value and sophisticated marketing.

BMW was able to make changes and adopt novel strategies in part because of its novel new structure. It was well connected within industry and with government at every level, but it also had a dominant private shareholder.

The management board members were never left in any doubt about the views of their main shareholder, and the bulk of them owed their appointment to him. They managed the business, but Quandt had an active and interventionist style and, for this reason, he often challenged management decisions and made them accountable. Quandt's influence and dominance ensured that BMW operated in a highly unusual way for a public company. Yet Quandt's involvement was at the level

of business strategy and business planning. His influence on the product came through his marketing or business vision. His judgments were not those of a carmaker, and in this way it is fair to say that BMW was not a company guided by a particular individual's vision or force of character in the way that Ford or Jaguar had been. As BMW prospered, Quandt retreated from direct intervention in management, confident that those he had put in place would act in the manner required.

The two-door variant of the *neu classe* appeared first as the 1600-2 in March 1966. At the time it is doubtful if BMW knew just how successful it would be. Not only did it come to figure prominently in the output tables, it also had an impact on the image of the company that was important for its success. Moreover, it was the two-door car that effectively penetrated export markets, doing so to a much greater extent than the four-door sedans. It is probably no exaggeration to say that the 2002 was the car that established BMW in the crucial U.S. market. Here was a small sedan that could outperform most sports cars and carried a degree of sophistication and practicality that the large V-8 muscle cars of the day lacked.

Once again BMW's success with the model owed something to its undoubted distinction and engineering

Far left: In addition to its obvious spoilers, decals, and racy alloy wheels, the Turbo was lowered to improve handling. Only 1,672 units were built in a 10-month production run.

Left: Although its 170-horsepower engine was considerably detuned, compared with the show car, it was still enough to give this boxy little two-door sedan serious urge. The top speed went up to 130 miles per hour and the 0–60 time came down to just 8 seconds, an astonishing figure for a 2.0-liter road car in the early 1970s. The primitive early turbocharger lacked the flexibility and response of modern units, and the boost could come in rather viciously, so driving it quickly required skill.

71

Inside, the Turbo featured sports seats, a smaller steering wheel, and extra instruments, including a boost gauge for the turbocharger.

On the first cars "Turbo" was written backward as an aggressive visual gimmick to warn lesser cars to move over on the autobahn. German critics decried it as a cheap gag, and BMW swiftly removed it.

quality, but also to the changing climate of the times. BMW perceived and responded to these changes, while many other manufacturers failed to appreciate that the world was changing around them.

During this period U.S. service personnel often spent time in Germany, and many young U.S. managers and executives spent at least some time in Europe. Mainstream U.S. motoring tastes remained very different from those of Europe, but there was an increasing number of affluent young U.S. buyers for whom European cars had a particular appeal. For BMW this sector was important and growing. The 2002 received rave reviews from the specialized and influential U.S. car magazines like *Road & Track* and *Car and Driver*. In fact, *Car and Driver* greeted the 1600 in 1967 as " the best small car we have ever driven." Even the demands of emissions legislation that was emerging at this time, and a hefty swing in the exchange rates against the dollar, were not sufficient to undermine enthusiasm for the car.

Not only were the 02 sedans correct in proportion, and a major advance over the bigger 1500/1800/2000 sedans in appearance, but they were a good 440 pounds lighter. In 2.0-liter form, even with a single carburetor, they could provide good performance. In injected form,

As an alternative to the Turbo, and a reaction to the oil crisis, BMW offered a pared-down economy version of the 02 with less chrome, a plainer interior, and a low-compression engine. It proved popular and remained on sale until 1977, overlapping with the 3 series.

as the Tii, they quickly gained a reputation as outstanding drivers' cars. They were quick, responsive and involving, with engines that, while never particularly quiet, were always willing to rev. Even today a good 2002 remains a pleasant car to drive. Over 400,000 were sold between 1968 and 1976, with relatively minor changes during the production run. Early cars tended to be more restrained in color, with whites and blues, but later years included brighter and more striking choices with bright yellows, greens, and a lurid 1970s orange. The car's interior also moved from a slightly claustrophobic dark plastic to lighter-colored fabric upholstery.

Alongside the sedan was the touring three-door wagon, which was offered with the full range of engine size options from 1971 to 1974. Despite its practicality, the wagon body failed to find favor with customers. Michelotti was responsible for reshaping the body into wagon format, and the result did not please everyone. Given the needs of the target market and the success achieved earlier in the United Kingdom by the Scimitar GTE, which offered a broadly similar sports estate configuration, it is difficult to see why the touring failed to achieve particular success. Whatever the reason, it was sufficient to dissuade BMW from venturing into the

wagon market again for many years. It was not until the late 1980s that a touring estate version of the 3 series was offered, albeit with a very much more elegant bodyshell, and the 5 series was not offered in wagon form until the 1990s.

Perhaps the wagon's failure is evidence of customers' sensitivity to their car's appearance. BMW has avoided exuberant styling flourishes, but its cars have always had a discreet, understated elegance. Proportion, materials, shape and color were all used carefully to create cars with a simple distinctive appearance. Company designers made few mistakes. Look at any of the models and it is difficult not to be impressed with the integrity and style. Perhaps the touring, with its large rear side windows and sloping tailgate, lacked the visual appeal necessary to attract the discriminating BMW buyer.

There were other 02 derivatives, including the 4,000-odd convertibles built by Baur. In typical German style, these were elegant convertibles with nothing of the improvised look that can sometimes accompany soft-top versions of factory enclosed cars. Without its roof, the BMW bodyshell lost a lot of its rigidity, as the door openings were large and the sills small and narrow. The convertibles built between 1968 and 1971 can hardly be regarded as ideal from an engineering standpoint. The later post-1971 versions with targa roof and distinctive roll hoop offer a much more acceptable solution providing reasonable rigidity—though tipping the scales 110.5 pounds heavier than the sedan.

THE 2002 TURBO—EUROPE'S FIRST PRODUCTION TURBO

Although the Americans were the first to experiment with turbocharging—witness the turboed Offenhauser racers at Indianapolis, and the Chevrolet Corvair Monza in the 1960s—it was BMW that launched the first turbo car in Europe, as a direct result of its racing activities from 1968. Porsche 911s beat the fuel-injected but normally aspirated 2002s in the 1968 European Touring Car Championship, and BMW needed to go harder.

With a rudimentary turbo setup—KKK blower mounted low down on the side of the engine—and pressurizing the fuel injection plenum chamber through a long pipe, the racing unit could produce up to 320 horsepower at a whacking 17-psi boost—but not for long. Still, the 2002 TIK (fuel injected with Kompressor) stayed together long enough to allow Dieter Quester to win four rounds of the 1969 championship, and for BMW to beat Porsche.

The road car shares the racer's turbo layout and there's still no intercooler, but in order to preserve the engine, compression is down to 6.9:1 from the Tii's 9.5:1. Boosting at a maximum of 7 psi over atmospheric pressure, the 1,900-cc chain-driven single overhead cam (SOHC) slant four kicks out 170 horsepower at 5,800 rpm. The sharp bump in the torque curve tells the tale of that all-or-nothing power delivery, with nearly 180 ft-lb appearing very suddenly at 4,000 rpm. Claimed performance figures were 0 to 60 miles per hour in under 7 seconds, 0 to 100 miles per hour in 21 seconds, and a top end of 130 miles per hour, just about coinciding with the redline in top gear. The factory claimed 19.5 miles per gallon fuel consumption. The car came with larger rims and flared arches along with front and rear roll bars and the option of a five-speed gearbox. The 2002 Turbo was clearly constructed as a homologation special, and its specification and option list was designed to ensure the eligibility of components deemed desirable for competition.

Nevertheless, the car attracted attention and enhanced BMW's image as a performance-car manufacturer. Yet despite its prominence in the Grand Prix turbo era, BMW was to move away from turbocharging as the way of extracting power and performance and concentrate on developing multivalve, naturally aspirated engines.

CHAPTER 4

BMW CARVES ITS NICHE: RESPONDING TO THE OPPORTUNITIES OF THE 1970s

The big BMW sedans marked BMW's reemergence in the executive class and were fast, refined cars. They tend to live in the shadow of the much more glamorous CS coupes but were much more important commercially.

Previous page: The 2500 and 2800 sedans of 1968 were aimed directly at Mercedes and were outstanding cars. The styling struck just the right note of modern, airy good taste.

By the later 1960s, BMW had become a confident company producing cars that were both well received and profitable. Parlaying that profit and confidence, BMW's ever forward-looking leadership introduced the new E21 range of large sedans. Confronting Mercedes directly in the market had always been a delicate issue for BMW, but the 2500 and 2800 were clearly competitors for the attractive but slightly old-fashioned sedans offered by Mercedes. The Mercedes l l4 series had been introduced early in 1968, yet somehow failed to appear new or fresh. Although fine cars, the Mercs had a slightly dated appearance with mechanical components that seemed already too familiar.

Of course the top-of-the-range Mercedes, the 3.5-liter V-8 300SEL, and the much more dramatic 6.3-liter 300SEL were very attractive, albeit very expensive cars. The 6.3 300SEL in particular was more than a match for the big BMWs in every way. Yet they were not the cars that made up the bulk of Mercedes' sales and hardly form an appropriate point of comparison. BMW was targeting the smaller 250S and 280S models, which, in comparison to the BMW, looked unwieldy and uninspired. Perhaps the closest rival was Jaguar's new XJ6, introduced at around the same time. Undercutting the BMW on price in every market, and providing performance, handling, and ride that could rival the BMW without difficulty, the Jaguar was an attractive proposition. The public doubt, of course, was about build quality, and the long Jaguar waiting lists still left ample room for BMW sales to those who were not too price conscious.

Once again BMW did not break any technical frontiers with its new sedan. In fact, it is hard to think of any feature of the car that was not already thoroughly familiar. A straight-six single overhead cam engine with alloy head, and MacPherson strut front suspension with semi-trailing arm rear made the car an obvious big brother to the 2000 range. Externally it shared a similar simple elegance. The decision to revert to a more conventional bonnet opening, as well as the extra length and slimness of the body sides, produced a car that was considerably more attractive than the four-door versions in the 2000 range.

Every element was so well executed that even today, the original big sedans still appear fresh and appealing. The 2500 was an adequate rather than exceptional performer and delivered only average fuel economy. A larger 2,800-cc model had more power with little difference in economy, but the later 3.0-liter, especially potent in injected form, transformed these capable cars into something with real response.

In accordance with its image, BMW marketed them as cars with an appeal first and foremost to the driver. Passengers and luggage all were well catered to, but a quick look in one of these sedans confirms it is centered around the driver. The very large instrument panel, housing an impressively dominant speedometer and rev counter set squarely in front of the driver, conveys the message. Unfairly overshadowed in enthusiasts' minds by the coupe version, these big sedans were fine cars that sold in large numbers and acquired a good reputation. The engine, in particular, was impressive in its smoothness and ability to rev. The heavily counterweighted seven-bearing crank ensured the smoothness and spun powerfully to 6,000 rpm and beyond. The engines proved able to meet the increasingly important U.S. emission regulations without air pumps and exhaust gas recirculation—though they had a healthy thirst for fuel.

Less successful perhaps was the three-speed ZF automatic transmission. Though reliable, it seemed to undermine the will and energy of the cars, and proved somewhat jerky in use. In part this was a result of the high-revving engine. The ZF unit was replaced by a better BorgWarner product when the 3.0-liter cars were introduced in 1971. But it was not until the early 1980s, with the advent of the four-speed automatics, that BMW finally got an automatic transmission that really matched the character of its cars. In fairness, few of its competitors' automatic offerings were any better. BMW's auto transmissions were singled out because the free-revving six and the sporting character of the cars encouraged drivers too expect more.

Bernhard Osswald, who became the new head of engineering after Fritz Fielder retired, laid the foundation for the new sedan. Anyone surprised at the appointment of a Ford executive as head of engineering at

Cabin styling didn't get much more modern or well planned in 1968, and this gave a taste of what was to come from BMW in the 1970s and 1980s.

The canted-over straight six was probably the best of its type in the late 1960s and even throughout the 1970s. The 2500 gave 150 horsepower and with the manual gearbox was capable of 120 miles per hour. Early carburetors, however, were troublesome to tune.

BMW MOTOR SPORT ACTIVITY

BMW has been involved in motorsport almost since its first days as a car manufacturer. Both the cars and the motorcycles have, to an extent, been promoted through participation in sporting events of one kind or another. In this way, BMW is no different from many other auto manufacturers. It is difficult to think of any manufacturer that has not at some point had a serious and sustained involvement with motorsport. Even General Motors, Nissan, and Volkswagen, perhaps the manufacturers who have shown least consistent participation in sporting events, have at various times promoted themselves in particular markets, and in particular sectors, through sport.

Unlike manufacturers such as Ford, BMW has not used its sporting activity to directly promote particular models. Instead the focus has been to project a wider image of the company's technical abilities. Talented individuals whose profile within motorsport gave them prominence have been trusted by the company to manage its sporting programs and deliver the required results. From early on, BMW developed the strategy of moving across categories of sport as its competitiveness changed. If BMW could not represent itself as a successful competitor, it would quickly withdraw from that area and find another where its intervention could produce a better result. Crucial to the management of these programs and the implementation of these strategies has been the role of various semi-independent teams and tuning firms.

This same policy was rigorously applied to both car and motorcycle competition. Like most manufacturers, BMW was also alert to the fact that it could derive the benefits of association with motorsport without a continued presence at a high level. By careful marketing, several years' activity could be followed by several years' limited involvement without undermining the association of the brand with a sporting image. This is the policy that has been adopted. It has the added value of attracting attention each time the company either moves into a series or withdraws from it. Alongside these carefully orchestrated entries and withdrawals would be the publicity, speculation, and review of past achievements that each change of policy would generate.

For manufacturers of luxury and prestige cars, racing rather than rallying tends to be the chosen competition route in recent years. BMW in particular has shown little interest in the form of motorsport that has helped to establish the sporting pedigree of more mundane makes such as Ford, Peugeot, Lancia and more recently, Japanese concerns such as Subaru and Mitsubishi. While the M3 and the earlier 2002 were used to an extent in rallying, the idea of a BMW covered in mud has little appeal to the BMW marketing people. While other marques may wish to use such a form of competition to symbolize the strength and robustness of their vehicles, BMW believed from early on that its engineering reputation was well enough established that the company did not need that kind of support.

Like many manufacturers, BMW had within its senior ranks at various times engineers, designers, and executives who had a personal interest and enthusiasm for motorsport. This was the case during the company's earliest competition activity, centering on the unlikely BMW 3/15.

In the Alpine Trial, the 328, driven by company employees in their private capacity, provided an important input into BMW competition achievement. Motorcycle racer Ernst Henne played an important role in the early years, and Alex von Falkenhausen and his engine engineering department devoted attention to the development of racing engines at a time when few resources were available in the company. Later, competitions department director Jochen Neerspach guided the company through some of its most active competition years, with the development of BMW Motorsport GmbH as an independent company within BMW.

Throughout the 1960s and 1970s, BMW used variants of its production sedans and coupes to good effect on the racing circuits of Europe. In competition BMW products tended to be best suited to long-distance races, in which the initially more highly developed models from other manufacturers might suffer reliability problems. Success or failure in these events reflected less on the inherent characteristics of the cars but much more on the abilities of competition managers to organize the necessary homologation of special race components. Initially BMW's instinct was to try to limit the extent to which it would have to devote resources to the production of special components. While the competition departments of BMC and Ford had elevated the practice of homologating the most unlikely components for their road cars to new heights, BMW was rather slower to adopt the practice. This is represented sometimes as BMW being concerned with retaining a close link between its racecars and production models. There was some

truth in this. Perhaps more important though was the fact that BMW, as a company that was growing very rapidly and could sell all it could produce, had little spare capacity for extraneous activity. Homologation involved demonstrating that significant numbers of cars had been made with the relevant components, and that the components were options available to the general public. BMW's engineering and production facilities were already fully stretched.

A second major element of BMW motorsport activity has been as an engine supplier. Initially perhaps BMW was less a supplier

than an inspiration. The hemi-headed 328 engine of the late 1930s was, as a result of the disruption caused by the war, to have an important role in competition. The 328s proved popular competition cars both before and after the war, while the engine subsequently was to appear rebadged as the Bristol unit. It found its way to England as part of war reparations. In this guise it was to be fitted to numerous sports racing and single-seater chassis, right up until the late 1950s. Developed in various stages and, according to Bristol, incorporating further metallurgical advances, the long-stroke 2.0-liter six-cylinder unit eventually was able to deliver high-power outputs. The engine was also used extensively in the rest of Europe in sports racing cars of various kinds.

Currently BMW supplies the 3.0-liter naturally aspirated V-10 engines that power the Williams cars. In Formula One, however, the BMW name is most associated with the short-lived but dramatic Turbo era of the 1980s. Under Neerspach's guidance, BMW initially agreed to produce a 1.5-liter turbocharged version of its existing Group 5 competition engine for Formula One use. It was a unit that could trace its origins back through the M12 Formula Two and sports car engine to the four-cylinder production engine used in the original 1500 saloon of the early 1960s.

The initial destination of the unit was to be the French Talbot Sport organization, to whom Neerspach, BMW's competitions director, had promised the engine. Others within BMW were less impressed with this option, and internal politics led to Neerspach's departure and replacement by Dieter Stappart as motorsport manager. Within a few weeks the agreement with Talbot was abandoned, and the engine was to be entrusted to Brabham, which at that time was owned by the boss of the Formula One Constructors Association, Bernie Ecclestone. The precise motivations behind this choice are now difficult to determine, but speculation suggested that the deal owed more than a little to BMW's desire to float the Procar series for its M1 model, which was to accompany each Grand Prix round courtesy of Ecclestone.

The BMW-Brabham link took time to develop. The turbo engine proved temperamental, and Brabham became sufficiently concerned about reliability to continue to use its existing V-8 Ford Cosworth naturally aspirated units long after BMW expected to see the results of its Cupertino. Yet in 1983 the BMW-powered Brabham finally came good, and after three wins and three second places, Nelson Piquet beat Renault and Alain Prost for the World Championship.

During the life of the BMW turbo engine, officially designated the M12/13, regulations and boost levels changed, but at various times the engine delivered over 1,000 horsepower in qualifying form. Eventually other chassis manufacturers had access to the BMW engine. Ligier, ATS, Benetton, and Arrows all at one time or another used the engine, but only Brabham achieved significant success. By 1987 the engine was no longer particularly competitive and BMW withdrew, though the engine remained in use, rebadged as a Megatron unit promoted by the Swiss engine tuner Henri Mader.

BMW enthusiasts are always pleased to recall that the cylinder blocks of these massively powerful units were alleged to be the familiar production block to be found in the base four-cylinder models of the time. Indeed the story goes that the company sourced used blocks, rather than new, as the period of use was deemed to have reduced internal stresses within the castings making them more robust. It is a story that it is now difficult to verify, but which is repeated with great regularity. It is also, of course, the kind of story that BMW would find beneficial and would play its part in spreading.

Throughout the 1990s BMW retained an involvement in auto racing in different series. As rules changed and the competitiveness of its cars varied, so did its strategy and involvement. Most of the sedan-based racing was managed through Schnitzer and centered on the M3 model.

BMW's recent return to Formula 1 as an engine supplier was announced in 1997, and the engines appeared in 2000. Unlike some other major manufacturers involved in Formula One, BMW's engines are genuine BMW products rather than constructed under contract by another company. Mercedes-Benz engines, for example, are designed and built under contract by United Kingdom–based Ilmor Engineering. Within a short period the BMW units have shown themselves competitive in the Williams chassis, and they will be unlucky if they do not achieve at least one win in the 2001 season, with more to come in future years.

BMW should remember that Ford was making the most dramatic changes in car production at this time. Ford was developing a range of cars that were to hold popular, profitable dominance in Europe for several decades.

Body design for the big sedans was undertaken in-house, and the cars look all the better for it. Coherence and simplicity mean that the cars are attractive from every angle and have aged well. Though conventional in their overall design concept, the cars, like the majority of new models, contained some interesting technical features. BMW was adept at maximizing the extent to which each design choice, however mundane, was represented as a major technical advance. In this way, through advertising and general approach to customers, BMW sought to position itself as a company offering technical innovation and leadership while, in fact, taking surprisingly few risks in design. By the late 1960s BMW brochures and press communications were full of

The original 2500/2800 sedans expanded into a whole range of cars, culminating in the long-wheelbase 3.3Li, BMW's retort to Mercedes' long-wheelbase S-Class models of 1972. Best of the bunch was the manual, fuel-injected 200-horsepower 3.0Si seen on the cover of this brochure.

The oddball 2000CS became the beautiful 2800CS when the new six-cylinder sedans emerged in 1968, retaining the old body from the pillars rearward but with a new handsome front end.

BMW 2.5 CS
A new dimension in driving pleasure for the most discerning: BMW 2.5 CS Coupé.

This is the rare "poverty spec" 2.5 CS produced in an attempt to keep sales of the CS coupe buoyant during the oil crisis.

carefully presented technical detail. The company always pitched at a level just above the heads of the intended readership, in a way that tapped into the contemporary respect for scientific knowledge. This, after all, was a time when a youthful generation saw science and engineering rationality as positive and unchallenged themes in all areas of life. BMW was perhaps uniquely sensitive, either by instinct or design, to these issues.

Trispherical combustion chambers, described helpfully in U.S. advertising as *Dreikugelwirbelwannen-brennraum*, was one feature brought to public attention more for the technical image that it created than perhaps for its success as an innovation. The company also highlighted the antidive front suspension, though it represented more a design choice than an innovation or breakthrough. Other manufacturers and models had incorporated a degree of antidive geometry in their front suspensions. BMW's distinctiveness involved its design

BMW sold 500 right-hand-drive English market CSLs, alongside the automatic CSA coupe, between 1972 and 1974. The cars had lightweight alloy doors, hood, and trunk panels.

choice rather than the means of executing it. That is, BMW engineers and marketing people knew how they wished the vehicle to respond and behave—that was the innovation and the achievement. The execution, engineering the vehicle to get that response, was a lesser and much less distinctive achievement.

Drive a BMW 2500 or 2800, or better still the later 3.0Si, and compare it with its competitors and it does feel different. With its large sedans selling at a premium price, BMW knew that the key to its success lay in giving the sedans a distinctive sporting character. Coherent marketing around this character and image were to bring BMW great success in future years. The big sedans were large and luxurious but also restrained and agile. BMW evolved a company with sufficient coherence and connectedness between its marketing, engineering, and production sections that the defined brand image could actually be translated into design features of the car. The

car was engineered to look, feel, and behave seamlessly in conformity with the brand image.

As the marque developed in later years, this learned behavior seemed to become instinctive. BMW always felt and looked right, always had a distinctiveness, and always seemed to find customers happy to pay high prices for its product. This was not an achievement of engineering but an achievement of management and organization. Long-wheelbase versions of the six-cylinder sedans were developed in response to the new SEL versions of Mercedes' 350 and 450 S class models. BMW loaded the flagship 3.3 Lia with all the options it could muster—including leather seats, some uncharacteristically ostentatious wood trim, and air conditioning—but somehow the BMWs never looked like convincing limousines next to the big Mercedes.

Alongside the sedans and using the same basic mechanical components, BMW introduced the 2800CS.

85

Inside the CSL featured Scheel lightweight bucket seats, but otherwise the dashboard and even the huge rather nonsporty steering wheel were much the same as the CS/CSi coupe.

Using an extended and more appealing version of the 2000CS shell, this was the first of a successful line of coupes that remain highly regarded in enthusiast circles. In terms of performance and road behavior they were little different from the sedans, being only marginally lighter and retaining similar spring rates. In fact, the coupe body with its thin pillars (and no central pillar) was not particularly rigid. Yet their attractive styling and practicality gave them great appeal. They were grand tourers with surprisingly few rivals. The large Mercedes coupes seem cumbersome and compromised in comparison, while the Porsche 911 demanded much

SORTING OUT THE CSLs

BMW built 1,000 "standard" 3.0 CSLs and 39 "Batmobiles," right? Wrong. In fact, there are many more "Batmobiles" than you'd think, and the so-called standard CSL came in three distinct variations.

The first cars—announced in May 1971—were real stripped-for-action road racers: thinner body panels; no front bumper; fiberglass rear bumper; racing latches on the hood; manual winding side windows, made from Plexiglas; and, of course, the alloy-skinned opening panels, all in the name of weight reduction. BMW even skimped on underbody rust protection and sound deadening. Along with some drastically cheaper interior trim, including thin carpets and lightweight Scheel bucket seats, 400 pounds were paired off the coupe. While the top speed wasn't much affected, acceleration was decisively quicker. The suspension was stiffened by Bilstein gas shocks with advanced progressive-rate springs, and the wheels were fat Alpina 7-inch alloys with chrome wheel arch extensions to keep them legal. Black accent stripes distinguished the *Leightgemetal* from the standard CS/CSi. The company built 169, all with left-hand drive. Originally fitted with the 2,985-cc carbureted in-line six, giving 180 horsepower, a slight bore increase in August 1972 gave 3,003 cc, which allowed the CSL to slip into 3.0-liter Group 2 competition. At the same time,

Bosch electronic injection replaced the twin Zenith carbs, and power rose to 200 horsepower. Brochures of the time quote a carburetor-fed 3,003-cc engine too. Just over 500 are reputed to have been built.

The British-specification right-hand-drive car was introduced in the United Kingdom in October 1972 and came with an "RHD City package" to appease fat-cat Brits who wanted the lightweight racer cache with none of the discomfort. Alloy panels, chrome wheel arch extensions, and bucket seats remained, but the United Kingdom CSL had proper bumpers, undercoating and sound deadening, standard coupe carpets, and even proper glass side windows, tinted and electrically operated. Power steering (sometimes with the standard 3.0-liter wheel, otherwise a sports alloy spoked job) returned too, as did softer CS suspension. The hood could be unlocked from inside the glove box, as on the all-steel CSL, although it was still manually propped rather than counterbalanced. The British importers (a separate operation from the factory in those days) took 500 CSLs and dropped the ordinary CSi at the same time, reckoning that buyers looking for the ultimate in BMW performance would take the lightweight, and lazy drivers the automatic, carburetor-engined CSa. In fact, the CSL was a slow seller. Prices were high—more than an Aston or greater involvement from the driver and delivered its performance in a more strident manner. Other rivals like the Jaguar E-type appeared cramped and unrefined in comparison. Introduced in 1968, their specification was updated alongside the sedans. By 1971 they had acquired the larger 3.0-liter engine, which could be had with either carbs or Bosch injection. Alongside the new 3.0-liter coupes came the CSL (see sidebar), a homologation special designed to make the marque stronger in competition.

As always with BMW, the limited production CSL acquired a special cache due to its relative rarity and the excitement generated by its alleged lightweight character.

In fact, the CSL remained a heavy car. Despite some alloy paneling and a more Spartan interior, the weight saving was not so substantial as to make a dramatic difference to performance. At best they were only 265 pounds lighter than the standard CSi, which in turn was less than 110 pounds lighter than the sedan. These were "lightweights" that still tipped the scales at nearly 3,100 pounds. In fact, a fair proportion of CSL production, particularly many of the cars that went to the United Kingdom, were still fitted with some of the heavier interior features like electric windows. Mechanically they remained similar to the standard CSi. Engines were allegedly given fractional bore increases

Jensen—and not everybody liked the awkward-to-get-into Scheel bucket seats or wanted to be bothered with the easily damaged alloy panels. The CSi reappeared before long and the last of the British batch of CSLs was sold in August 1974.

Special RHD Equipment for Great Britain. BMW 3.0 CSL

The 3.2 liter CSL—"Batmobile" to you and me—was announced in August 1973. It was left-hand drive only and had a bigger 3.2-liter (actually 3,153-cc) 206-horsepower engine to homologate the 84-millimeter stroke used on the 3.5-liter works racing coupe. It was still badged 3.0-liter.

The car used the lightweight shell (initially available only in Polaris silver or Chamonix white with optional motorsport stripes) as before, with alloy doors and bonnet, but—to take the weight and downforce of the rear wing—the trunk lid was steel with fitting for the spoiler. And yes, the spoiler (or racing kit) was packed away in the trunk on cars sold in West Germany, where such appendages were never legal. There was a deep front spoiler, a roof hoop spoiler just above the rear window, a small lip spoiler on the edge of the bootlid, and rubber "splitters" on the front fenders. Lighter single-plate side glass was used and—like the previous German-spec CSLs—"Batmobiles" had fixed rear quarter windows. Manual steering and Bilstein gas-pressure shocks with three alternative levels of hardness meant that the 3.2-liter CSL didn't need an anti-roll bar.

Around 100 of these cars were built, but not all had their racing kits fitted, and owners could opt for the "town kit" with standard bumpers, softer suspension, and even air conditioning if required.

There was a last batch—built in 1974–1975—of unofficial series two "Batmobiles" with minor differences like a three-fin rear bat-wing and a driver's seat with an adjustable backrest. Fifty-six of these were built.

For the collector, the "Batmobile" CSL is the ultimate prize. Only a handful were built using the "standard" CSL as a base but with flamboyant aerodynamic aids.

to bring them up to 3,003 cc in order to move them into a competition class where victories were more likely. Whether this increase was a real one, or whether it merely represented an increase in the tolerance declared for the purposes of homologation remains an open question. Later, a more substantial increase in stroke brought them up to 3,153 cc.

This was the era in which motorsport once again looked to aerodynamics for competitive advantage. This time, however, designers looked not just for a slippery shape, but for means to generate downforce to aid vehicle grip and handling at high speeds. Formula One cars of the period became festooned with large, high-mounted wings. The CanAm cars of the period used various airfoils and skirts in addition to large wings in an attempt to minimize drag and maximize downforce.

BMW followed suit in the early 1970s with its race CSL coupes, which quickly became known as "Batmobiles" as a result of the fins and wings they began to sprout. Most distinctive were two longitudinal fins along the front fenders, along with a very large rear spoiler suspended from two sideplates.

These very visible features attracted notice but perhaps more important was the range of competition equipment that BMW Motorsport developed. These speed goodies included a 24-valve cylinder head and a special crank without the extensive counterweighting featured on production models.

Most manufacturers of this period had motorsport divisions producing homologation specials and a wide range of exotic performance equipment. You could buy exotic alloy eight-port heads for Minis, magnesium bell housings for Escorts, limited-slip differentials for Renaults, and straight-cut gearboxes for Volvos, to cite just a few examples from the period. That BMW produced similar items for its vehicles is in no way surprising, given the increasing role that motorsport was to have in manufacturers' marketing plans. The extent of modifications available at this time was extensive, and anyone believing that the racing CSL of the mid-to-late 1970s bore much relation to its road-going partners is misguided. The gear-driven camshafts, dry sump lubrication, and numerous other modifications these cars featured were developed by race engineers for competition, not for road use and mass production.

The CSL coupes initially were not strong competitors, but after development they began to score some success in Europe by 1973, and later in the United States. Both Alpina and Schnitzer ran coupes

This rear spoiler was packed in the trunk when the car was delivered. BMW left it to the owner to decide if he or she wanted to be that much of a showoff. Note the plastic bumpers and chrome wheel arch extensions.

BMW ADVERTISING

BMW has become the favorite case study for those trying to understand successful marketing. Using the notion of a niche market, the company has successfully projected itself and its products as among the most sought after. In marketingspeak, they have consistently sought to project the same four core values since the mid-1960s: technology, quality, performance, and exclusivity.

In the United Kingdom the company has used the same advertising agency since the late 1970s, WCRS, and the campaigns that have emerged have always focused on one or more of the company's key core values that BMW wishes to keep in the public's mind. More recently a fifth value, described as "driving," has been added to the list. "Driving" is the phrase used to project the notion that BMW's now-distinctive (some would say anachronistic) rear-wheel-drive configuration offers the driver an enhanced experience, compared with other performance saloons. While enthusiasts will acknowledge the benefits of rear-wheel drive for driver enjoyment, the simplistic assertions about this being in some way a "natural" configuration with the car "pushed into the corner" are embarrassing.

For many years BMW campaigns have focused on the cars themselves, rather than characters, story lines, or locations as in many car ads. One analysis of this has suggested this is because people always suggest an element of fallibility while BMW is anxious to focus all aspects of the ads on the brand values. For example, if the vehicle is shown in front of a building, that building's design and presentation will reflect BMW's ideas about technology and quality; if the vehicle is shown on a road, it will be a well-maintained road, with smooth surfaces and manicured edges.

Film likewise has provided an opportunity for exposure for BMW. Use of BMW models in James Bond films, for example, offers benefits to BMW in the form of publicity rather than direct product advertising. It raises public awareness of the marque, and the latest model, without necessarily directly affecting target purchasing groups. The Z3 was used as James Bond's car in *Golden Eye,* the decision to use it in this role affected by the fact that the Z3 was produced in the United States and BMW had recently become involved with Rover. These developments were perceived as giving the car the international character that the film producers wanted. Extensive cross promotion agreements were put in place. Later the Z8 was used in the recent Bond film, *The World Is Not Enough.*

BMW at Dungeness Nuclear Power Station.

The 132mph BMW 3.0Si.
When it's a matter of power.

Power not for its own sake, but for what it can achieve. For those with a natural regard for power look beyond the image of ownership and appreciate a BMW for its true value. BMW 3.0Si provides opportunities to overtake confidently when others must cautiously hold back. Its 220 brake horsepower engine retains latent reserves : in hazardous situations Apollo-like acceleration is readily on hand to speed you clear. The BMW 3.0Si has electronic fuel injection precisely-metered by its own compact computer. With heated rear window, dual circuit braking, fitted headrests all-round and laminated windscreen all fitted as standard equipment. Unlike some luxury three-litres, the BMW 3.0Si isn't an extravagant decoration. It's a powerful Sports Saloon that earns its keep in the nuclear power age.

Unbeatable BMW present a range of Sports Saloons starting at £1899

es of the BMW range : 102 mph (Autocar test report) BMW 1602 : £1899 – 113 mph (Autosport) BMW 2002 : £2145 – 106 mph (Motor) BMW 2000 Touring : £2349 – 119 mph (Autosport) BMW 2002tii : £2495 – 121 mph (Autocar) BMW 2500 : £3299 – 127 mph (Autocar) BMW 3.0S : £4030 – 132 mph (Autocar) BMW 3.0Si : £4299 – 125 mph BMW 3.0CSA : £6199, 141 mph BMW 3.0CSi : £6199.
ZF Sports Automatic Transmission optional on the BMW 2002 model at £219 and the BMW 2500, and 3.0S models at £269.
Prices shown are recommended retail prices including P.T.

BMW Concessionaires GB Limited, BMW House, Chiswick High Road, London, W.4. Tel : 01-995 4651, London Showroom, N.A.T.O., Diplomatic and Export Office : 56 Park Lane, London, W.1. Tel : 01-439 6881

ALPINA—BMW'S FAVORED TUNER

Alpina is perhaps the name most closely associated with modified BMWs. Concentrating on the marque since the mid-1960s, Alpina developed as a business offering sophisticated enhancement of even BMW's most exciting models.

The emphasis was upon the complete transformation of the vehicle, rather than the addition of odd bits and pieces. Though Alpina is independent of BMW, the two companies maintained close links during this period, and Alpina was clearly looked upon with greater favor than most other BMW tuners. More recently companies such as Schnitzer and Prodrive have been involved in competition preparation of BMWs, and these links have to some extent weakened Alpina's hold both on the market and on BMW. Nevertheless Alpina, previously a company involved in producing and selling typewriters and office equipment, has had an important role in BMW history.

Founded by Burkhard Bovensipen, the company began by offering twin-carb conversions for the *neu classe* sedans and received the tacit approval of both BMW's research and development department and, perhaps more importantly, Paul Hahnemann, the influential marketing chief at BMW. As BMW models developed, so did Alpina's range of offerings. The 02 series offered special opportunity. For the 2002, BMW developed special engines, blueprinted and balanced, with different cam profile and pistons along with the familiar enhanced induction and exhaust systems. Alpina-modified BMWs featured strongly in competition, both at the international level but also, perhaps just as importantly for the company's profile, at smaller local events throughout Europe.

By 1973 an Alpina-developed 2002Tii was offered as a complete, fully developed model in its own right. Success of this model and the changing market climate led Bovensipen to move increasingly toward the provision of complete cars. Alpina's naturally aspirated 2002 was a more pleasant car to drive than the factory's own 2002 turbo model, with more progressive power delivery. Indeed, Alpina had already had a hand in the birth of the 2002. It quickly yielded to the temptation to insert a 2,000-cc engine into the original 1600. Alpina's efforts, along with the advocacy of U.S. importer Max Hoffman, encouraged the factory to develop its own version, which became the 2002. Alpina also pioneered the use of Kugelfischer mechanical fuel injection with the engine, offering an injection kit for the carbureted 2002 toward the end of 1970 before the factory was to travel the same route and offer the 2002Ti.

Alpina produced modified versions of each of BMW's new models, each one offering enhanced performance and handling at a significant markup in price.

They included turbo versions of the 5 series cars, configured both in single- and twin-turbo form. They also found a small but enthusiastic market for a version of the large 7 series sedan, though in this case it was restricted to the United Kingdom market—where the 745i was not available—and was constructed by Alpine United Kingdom agent Frank Sytner and designated the B10. B12 versions of the V-12 750 saloon and 850 coupe were also offered, with capacity increased to 5.7 liters and the price tag of the B12 850 reaching around 250,000 deutsch marsks in 1994.

More recently, Alpina's relationship with BMW has given rise to a new concept—the ultrahigh-performance diesel. Introduced at the 1999 Geneva show, the Alpina D10 bi-turbo was dubbed the Super diesel, with a top speed in excess of 155 miles per hour. The D10 featured second-generation common rail fuel injection and twin turbos with adjustable turbine geometry.

The 2002 Turbo (foreground) and CSL coupe sum up BMW at its most aggressive and virile in the 1970s.

in racing and developed extensive preparation and aftermarket performance businesses on the back of their success. Both companies were to be intimately associated with the development of performance BMWs in subsequent years.

Nearly 250,000 of the big sedans and coupes were produced in a production run that lasted from 1968 to 1977. The biggest seller was the 2500, with 90,000 produced, while coupe sales totaled nearly 30,000.

The famed CSL accounted for around 1,000 examples. Many were exported and all sold at prices that carried handsome profit margins for the company. Not only were the cars sold at premium prices, but the long production run with little change, along with a design that was easy to produce, meant that margins were good. BMW had entered the virtuous circle where success breeds further success, and profit brings further profit.

Rubber "splitters" on the tops of the fenders were said to aid airflow but were not much help when you wanted to work on the engine. "Vents" on the sides of the wings are dummies.

All "Batmobiles" were injected and bored out slightly to give 3,153 cc for homologation purposes. The engine's 206 horsepower gave 140 miles per hour and 0–60 in 7 seconds, but with total docility and reasonable economy.

The racing Group 2 CSL coupe was the basis of the first of BMW's "art" cars. Alexander Calder, the American sculptor who invented the "Batmobile," was responsible for the CSL.

CHAPTER 5

THE NEW GENERATION: 3, 5, 6 AND 7 SERIES

Previous page: The 1980 M535i was the first of the performance-orientated 5 series models and was the first official M-badged road car.

Only modest spoilers differentiated the M535 visually from lesser species of 5 series, but the car also featured up-rated brakes, Recaro seats, and mildly up-rated suspension—its handling could still be lurid. This car, now owned by Tim Hignett of L&C BMW in the United Kingdom, was a press demonstrator.

By the early 1970s, the four-door 2000 sedans were showing their age against the competition. While the 02 models had become a runaway success, both at home and abroad, sales of the four-door sedan now lacked buoyancy.

It was against this background that the new 5 series four-door sedan was to be developed. BMW shaped the E12 into the 5 series at a time when the company was developing rapidly and had become acknowledged as a leader in the production of high-quality performance cars.

BMW advanced several elements of its philosophy in producing and developing the E12. First it designed the car to accommodate a very wide range of engines. All of BMW's available power units—from a mundane 1.8-liter four-cylinder to a 220-horsepower 3.5-liter six—were to find their way into that shell. Secondly, using conventional, well-proved engineering and components, the company produced a car that was better than the sum of its parts. Throughout the 5 series there is an appealing coherence in design.

Introduced in 1972 as the 520 and 520i, the new car drew heavily on its predecessor for major mechanical components and layout. The new series used the same familiar four-cylinder slant four with the same MacPherson strut front suspension and semi-trailing arm rear end. What was different was a much more modern and sophisticated bodyshell. Not only was the new car required to register improvement over its predecessor against all the usual measures of performance, it was also required to be a major advance in terms of refinement and feel.

These were the areas in which BMW felt it could offer the added value that was at the core of the company's pricing and marketing strategy. The opportunity to develop the new car also meant an opportunity to construct a bodyshell that was not only more modern, but simpler and more profitable to make.

BMW made major investments in the late 1960s and early 1970s to expand and upgrade the production facilities. The company purchased Glas in 1966 and quickly incorporated its plants. Throughout the early 1970s BMW spent more than 2 thousand million marks each year on plant expansion and upgrading at Munich, Dingolfing, and Landshut. The 520, assembled at the Dingolfing plant, marked the beginning of a new generation of BMW models.

Introduced in Europe in 1972 with 2.0-liter four-cylinder engines, the new 5 series appeared at a time when manufacturers were becoming much more constrained by legislative initiatives. Because of U.S. safety and environmental controls, BMW did not launch the 5 series in the U.S. market until 1975. Even then it was a specially developed model with a 3.0-liter engine and a range of additional features to meet the plethora of new regulations.

In the 5 series, BMW introduced new standards of ride comfort and noise suppression. For some it represented a softening of the marque's sporting edge; the extra weight of the new shell meant performance of the original 2.0-liter cars was adequate rather than startling. Against its rivals it was impressive. The Paul Bracq–styled body was neat and compact, rather than particularly attractive in its original form. (It wasn't until the early 1980s' face-lift with its raised boot line that the lines really looked right.) Still, in comparison to its rivals, it appeared functional and classy. As with all BMWs, the large glass area and the delicate treatment of window pillars and scuttle imparted a lightness and elegance to the shell that was lacking in other early 1970's designs.

In terms of chassis engineering perhaps the 5 series' greatest rival among mass producers came from Ford with their new European 1971 Granada range. Both cars shared similar strut front suspension and independent semi-trailing arm rear ends. Both were catering to the successful middle class, but where the Ford looks gross and cumbersome, the BMW looks neat and agile. Underneath the skin, the Ford chassis performed well, offering ride and handling that was not that far from the standards set by BMW. Steering feel on the Ford was less successful, but its image and marketing was crude in comparison to the increasingly sophisticated campaigns launched by BMW. For BMW the task was to maintain the image of exclusivity at a time when it was growing from a small producer serving niche markets to a considerably larger operation whose products were now a common sight. BMW was conscious that its particular market sector had become attractive to others.

Perhaps BMW's most important competitor was Audi, which had emerged a few years earlier. In 1968, Audi introduced the 100LS and 100GL sedans. These were cars that in any objective evaluation posed a real threat to BMW. They shared a quality feel, had the same image of rational engineering, and were styled with restraint and care. The original Audi 100 series made BMW's existing 2000 models look old-fashioned, and they played their part in stimulating the development of the 5 series. Audi was more innovative and adventurous in engineering than the innately conservative BMW.

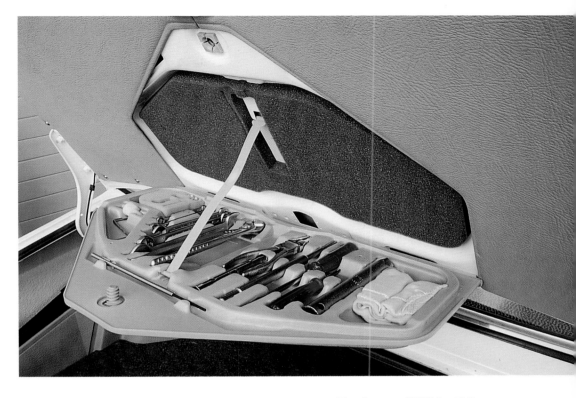

The famous BMW tool kit mounted in the trunk lid was a feature first found on the six-cylinder sedans and coupes of the late 1960s.

The M535i used a standard 3.5-liter engine taken from the 6 series coupe, complete with five-speed gearbox. No automatics were built. Over the years, BMW's Motorsport department built several uprated one-offs based on stock models for board members and special customers.

The first 5 series was one of BMW's longest-lived models. The basic shape ran from 1972 to 1988. This is the ultimate example, the twin-cam Motorsport-engined M5 of 1985.

The 5 series was an important new mainstream sedan, replacing the new class. It heralded a new model numbering system based on 1930s practices: 5 was the series, while the other two numbers denoted engine size—which initially was a carbureted or injected 2.0-liter four carried over from the previous model.

For example, Audi pioneered front-wheel drive in this sector of the market long before it was fashionable. Just when that innovation became widely popular, it raised the stakes and introduced the Quattro, with four-wheel drive. Alongside this, Audi gave its 1983 models a new aerodynamic bodyshell—in sharp contrast to BMW, which pursued performance through larger and more powerful engines. By the 1990s, Audi was exploring aluminum construction with the new A8. Audi also made careful use of competition—through the Quattro rally success—to enhance its image and marketing as a technology leader.

Curiously, Audi always sought to produce vehicles with engines smaller than buyers might expect. The original, and quite large, 100 series was powered by a 1,700-cc four, while throughout the 1970s and 1980s Audi offered models with engines no larger than 2.2 liters. BMW, on the other hand, required little excuse to put larger and more powerful engines into the existing bodyshells, producing increasingly exciting cars.

Audi, while producing cars with excellent road manners and an ability to cover ground exceptionally quickly, somehow developed a reputation for blandness and lack of driver involvement. In part, these perceptions were orchestrated and repeated by unimaginative road testers for whom the BMW formula of tail-happy

rear-wheel-drive sedans had an instinctive appeal. Whatever the cause, although Audi very successfully penetrated the sector and produced some very fine cars, it was less successful at projecting the kind of image that BMW had achieved.

The 5 series had its competitors, but it was clearly a car in tune with its times. Offering reasonable performance with the 2.0-liter four, it was joined within a year by the 525, using the 2.5-liter six-cylinder engine from the big sedans. By 1975 BMW offered a 528, and in the early 1980s began offering injected 3.5-liter units in the 5 series bodyshell.

As capacity increased so did performance. With the 525, the gain in torque and refinement was perhaps more noticeable than outright power and quite a few competing models could match the car's performance. The big six-cylinder unit was quite heavy, and the 525 weighed in well over 220 pounds heavier than its four-cylinder counterpart. The American market 3.0-liter 530 was heavier still, with a curb weight of over 3,300 pounds. Still, the cars sold well both in Europe and the United States, where they were regarded as a "compact" with real performance and driver appeal compared to offerings from U.S. manufacturers, which were at a particularly low ebb at the time. By 1977 even the 2.0-liter 5 series was to get a new six-cylinder engine, designated the M60. This was a

short-stroke unit with closely spaced cylinders built with a very clear focus on cost. A cast-iron, rather than forged, crank was used and unlike all previous BMWs, the engine featured a belt-driven cam. More modern casting techniques allowed engine weight to be kept down, so it was not that much heavier than the four it replaced. Overall the small sixes worked out about 44 to 66 pounds heavier than their predecessors when installed, and only about 80 percent of the weight of the big sixes.

The M60 cannot be regarded in technical terms as a great engine. For the motorsport fraternity it offered little potential as it was built to stringent cost controls and had none of the strength reserves that appeal to engine tuners. In service it worked satisfactorily, delivering good fuel economy in injected form and offering reasonable service life.

Responding to Audi's success with the layout, BMW built several 5 series cars with a transverse M60 engine installation and front-wheel drive. It rejected the design after testing. When planning the M60 engine, BMW decision-makers also considered a five-cylinder engine, similar to Audi's, but rejected it because the inherently better-balanced six-cylinder units could be built at similar or lower cost.

Though successful, the 5 series was just part of a new range of cars that were to shape BMW's fortunes in

With the introduction of the revised E28 5 series in 1984 came a showier M535i with spoilers and skirts but no extra performance—the engine was still a stock 3.5-liter single-cam straight six. This gray import European-specification car is owned by Michael Dennison of Bavarian Professionals, and has been fitted with later-spec M5 wheels.

This was more like it—the "real" M5 of 1984 to 1987, with less show and more go. Only modest front and rear spoilers and a discreet M badge front and rear told other drivers this was BMW's ultimate Q-ship. This car is owned by L&C BMW in Kent, England.

future years. Over 45,000 new 520s were sold in 1973, even though they were priced at over 15,000 deutsch marks before buyers added anything from the options list. Meanwhile the aging 02 series continued in production with little sign of a downturn in sales. They were particularly successful in the United States, where domestic manufacturers had responded to new safety and emissions legislation with vehicles that had little appeal to enthusiastic drivers. Safety considerations were also threatening the two-seat open sports car in these markets, and the 2002 sedan, with its impressive performance and

established reputation, prospered accordingly. Influential U.S. magazines like *Road & Track* and *Car and Driver* had taken the BMW to their hearts, promoting its virtues and ridiculing the domestic products.

In export markets other factors were moving in BMW's favor. In particular, all their competitors in the British, French, and Italian motor industries were in one kind of crisis or another. The Italian motor industry, increasingly concentrated in the hands of Fiat, was largely abandoning claims on the executive and luxury market and concentrating, very successfully, on challenging

Ford in small-car production. In France a lack of investment and idiosyncratic design prevented the car industry from effectively penetrating export markets with cars in the larger and more expensive price bracket. Perhaps more importantly from BMW's point of view, the French manufacturers seemed to be deliberately avoiding the performance-car market.

Peugeot, for example, introduced the 504 sedan in 1967, a car that could well have rivaled the BMW 5 series with a little development and some imaginative reworking. But the French manufacturer made no attempt to develop it for this sector of the market. Meanwhile the British motor industry, where Jaguar, Triumph, and Rover had traditionally sought to serve markets that overlapped BMW's, was in disarray. Not only did these manufacturers struggle on with poorly developed versions of cars which, in the case of Rover and Triumph, were now outdated, but they also fell victim to changing expectations of build quality.

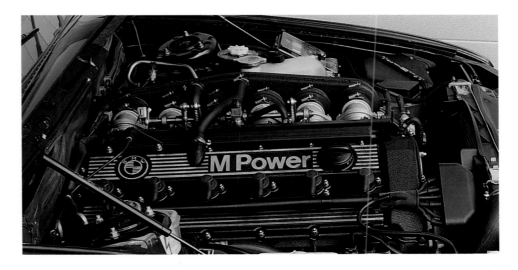

Under the hood lurked BMW's 24-valve Motorsports' straight six, delivering a smooth 286 horsepower for 153 miles per hour and 0–60 in 6 seconds.

PAUL BRACQ

Born in 1933, Paul Bracq is a Frenchman who made his name at Mercedes in the late 1950s and early 1960s. His most famous creations were the roof design of the 230SL and the whole body of the big 600 limousine, though he had input on quite a few of the models produced in the 1960s. He returned to France in 1967 to work for Brissonneau and Lotz, and had some involvement in the design of the TGV for the French Railways. Shortly after he found himself back in Germany in 1970 as head of styling for BMW, replacing Wilhelm Hoftmeister.

He was almost immediately involved in the design of the 3 and 5 series BMWs and the prototypes of the 6 and 7 series models, which emerged in 1976 and 1977. "I was unhappy with the first 7 series," he said. "It was too high, looked too heavy. I wanted something more like a Jaguar. I fought with the concept office—Bob Lutz in other words—but then came the fuel crisis, Lutz left, and I decided to return to France as well."

Bracq, along with many of the personalities involved in design at BMW, acquired something of an aura about themselves and their work. Rarely described merely as a car designer but also as a painter and sculptor, Bracq appears to have been, like Goertz, an able advocate for his own abilities and achievements. His name inevitably seems familiar in the world of art, but there is a mischievous rumor that more than one impressionable journalist has confused his artistic achievements with those of George Braque, one of the founders of cubism and a dominant figure in twentieth-century art.

Paul Bracq's artistic output has been more limited. He has been an able illustrator and painter of cars, and it is in that area of art that his achievements have been recognized. His stay at BMW was followed by a period as chief interior designer for Peugeot, where he remained until 1996. Perhaps his most famous BMW is the one that never went into production, the 1972 Turbo, a flamboyant mid-engined show car with a flame-red nose and tail.

Recaro leather seats gave the necessary body-hugging assurance needed at the kind of cornering speeds the M5 could generate, thanks to its better-sorted chassis.

A North American–specification M5 owned by Regan Clarke.

Further down the market, Japanese cars such as Datsun and Toyota were transforming expectations about reliability and quality control. Those paying significantly more for their vehicle were no longer prepared to tolerate vehicles delivered with multiple defects and regular component failures. Although the Japanese vehicles were largely uncompetitive in terms of road behavior and styling, they were increasingly attractive for their reliability and the equipment they offered. The British midrange manufacturers were caught up in a frenzy of amalgamations and restructuring that did little for their effectiveness as businesses. Cars that were complex and expensive to build, assembled in plants with outdated tooling and facilities, and sold through dealerships under threat of closure all conspired to ensure that no British marque was likely to threaten BMW's new-found dominance. BMW benefited from these raised quality expectations while remaining, for the time being, insulated from competition as its discerning customers did not regard the new Japanese models as sufficiently distinguished.

BMW and the Search for Fuel Economy

The early 1980s saw a considerable rise in fuel costs and a corresponding concern about vehicle fuel consumption. Any carmaker, however insulated by an affluent customer base, had to begin thinking about these issues. BMW's response is interesting technically, and also reveals its strengths as a company.

Most manufacturers approached fuel economy in piecemeal fashion. They axed the large ends of their range, added gimmicky vacuum gauges to their cars calling them "economy" meters, and in some cases extended gearing inappropriately to make fuel consumption figures look better. In the longer term manufacturers commenced research that was to have considerable impact on design, but in the short term they had little to offer.

BMW was one of the few manufacturers able to respond in a coherent way, despite the fact that its customers were the ones least likely to be influenced by fuel price changes. Because BMW had portrayed itself as at the forefront of technical excellence, it had to show its capacity for technical leadership in the area of fuel economy. In 1974 it had responded to oil price increases with downrated 2.5-liter CS coupes that customers avoided. By the 1980s crisis, it responded with a more

The 2002 was replaced in 1975 by the 3 series—larger, heavier, and roomier, but perhaps not as sporty as the car it superseded. Initially there were only four-cylinder versions of 1.6, 1.8, and 2.0 liters but the 320 and 323i emerged in 1977 with a new small six. The 323, pictured, was regarded as a true successor to the 2002 Tii. This car is owned by Tim Hignett of L&C BMW.

The 3 series was a successful follow-up to the 02 cars. Here the first- and second-generation 323i two-door sedans show how the styling evolved.

interesting development that came to fruition initially in the United States as the 2.7-liter 528e, introduced in 1981, and later as the European 525e. Both of these models sought to combine high performance and excellent drivability with significant gains in fuel economy and emissions. One part of the package was an extensively reworked engine, which came to be identified with the designation "ETA."

In addition to engine changes, BMW engineers carefully reworked the gearing and transmission options to suit the character of the car. This resulted in one of the more successful attempts to produce a more economical vehicle, and influenced subsequent design thinking within the company. With the ETA concept, engineers attempted to minimize internal friction and power loss and optimize the engine speed for the type of use to which the vehicle was likely to be subjected. Instead of reducing engine size, BMW proposed to use a large engine to maximize torque but run it at low revs to

minimize friction losses. This route to economy also has the advantage of producing a car that is attractive and relaxing to use.

Internally, friction losses were reduced in a variety of ways. The low rev requirements of the engine allowed weaker valve springs, which in turn produced less valve gear loading, allowing a reduction in the number of camshaft bearings from seven to four. Low revs allowed a reduction in valve overlap, while long intake tracts were used to assist with cylinder filling. Even ring tension was examined in an attempt to reduce internal frictional losses, while the compression ratio was raised. For the United States, where lower-octane unleaded gasoline was already the norm in the early 1980s, it could only go up to 9:1. European markets, offering gas of 98 or 99 octane, allowed the use of an 11.0:1 ratio. Engineers also introduced more sophisticated engine management, with a new Bosch Motronic system incorporating a fuel cutoff and a 5,000-rpm rev limit. The engine was linked to a five-speed Getrag gearbox with an overdrive fifth, or a four-speed automatic with a torque converter lock-up feature to minimize power loss.

The high torque available from the engine at very low revs allowed it to pull a top gear offering over 30 miles per hour per thousand revs. The result was an economical car that still retained the features that made BMWs enjoyable.

The 525e and 528e were the only models specifically designated to utilize the ETA engine, yet its importance should not be overlooked. Each model revision in the BMW line-up incorporated some of the lessons learned in the ETA's development. As a consequence, each new-generation BMW offered enhanced economy when compared with its predecessor.

Alongside ETA development, BMW began work on various diesel projects. Though largely unknown in either the United States or United Kingdom, the turbo-diesel 5 series BMWs became an important part of the company's 1980s model range in Europe. In the mid-1970s, diesels accounted for 40 percent of Mercedes sales, and many parts of Europe embraced diesel cars in the 1980s. For BMW, developing a diesel engine was therefore a logical, perhaps even overdue, step.

Part of the company's problem in going forward was a familiar one—shortage of factory capacity. Demand for existing models and the rapid growth of the company had left BMW with little or no space capacity in which to make new developments. Accordingly, in 1979 BMW entered a joint venture with the Austrian Steyr-Daimler-Puch AG concern to produce diesel engines in a new purpose-built plant. These engines were destined both for their own vehicles and to be sold to other manufacturers. The partnership produced engines for Ford USA that also appeared as options in the 1984 Lincoln model range. The BMW 524td, with a 2.4-liter turbocharged diesel engine, appeared in the middle of 1983. At the time it was hailed as the fastest diesel sedan, with a maximum speed in excess of 110 miles per hour and reasonable acceleration. It impressed most observers with its refinement when compared to other diesel-engined cars of the time. BMW achieved this performance and

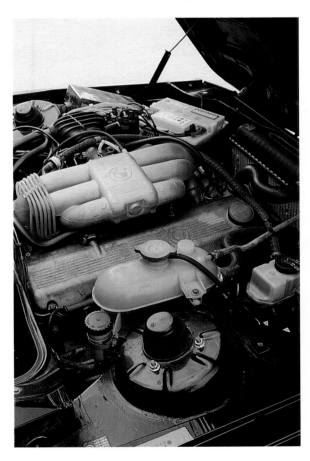

The smooth, sprightly M60 straight six has not proven to be the strongest of BMW engines, but was acclaimed for its performance in the 323i.

The dashboard repeated the themes explored in the 5 series, wrapping the important controls around the driver. BMW dashboards to this day are based around the same idea.

refinement not just through the new engine but, in typical BMW fashion, from the careful manner in which it was fitted to the car.

The engine itself was thoroughly conventional, following modern diesel practice. Based on the M60 block and using an alloy head, it was not dissimilar to diesel units offered by Volvo, Peugeot, and Citroen. For its size, it was quite high revving, with a governed maximum of 5,000 and peak power coming at 4,800 rpm. With a flat torque curve and quite high levels of turbo boost (peaking at 0.8 bar) the engine gave the 524td sufficient power to make it a success in the market and a worthy addition to the BMW range. If the engine itself was conventional, the installation in the 5 series shell was particularly neat and competent, with great attention paid to suppression of vibration, noise, and harshness.

Today's customers, particularly in the United Kingdom and Europe, expect high-revving sophisticated diesels to be offered in every manufacturer's range. They are accustomed to turbocharged intercooled diesels that can rival gasoline vehicles in performance, yet still deliver excellent economy. In the early 1980s this was not the expectation. Diesels were still seen as sluggish vehicles prone to noise and vibration. Both Citroen and Peugeot had led the way in challenging these negative expectations to some degree. Peugeot's fine turbocharged 505 and 604 models showed what was possible, but even Mercedes diesels were regarded—with justification—as slow and noisy, while those from Ford and General Motors were simply unpleasant. Against this background, BMW unleashed the 524td, which played its part in transforming the way diesels were regarded in Europe.

The partnership with Steyr proved less successful. BMW bought out its partner after some degree of disagreement only two years after they started the venture. While BMW continued to offer a diesel option, the company didn't sustain its early enthusiasm for diesel

A factory shot of the Baur-built 3 series cabriolet, featuring much the same principles as the old 02 Cabriolet with a Targa roof with an integral rollover bar and a folding cloth section behind.

development, leaving Peugeot and Citroen as technical leaders in this area. BMW made fewer diesels as a proportion of vehicle output than did Mercedes or most other carmakers.

BMW management seemed to have decided that diesel-powered vehicles were to be tolerated rather than cherished in the company's model range. In some ways this may have been a product of the conservatism that increasingly came to characterize BMW in the late 1970s and 1980s. A company growing as rapidly as BMW with a successful product line and satisfied customers has little inclination to make radical departures. A company as sensitive to the market as BMW knows also the value of consistent brand image and coherent product strategies in a sector so often influenced by imitation and fashion.

The Introduction of the New 3 Series

Alongside 5 series development, BMW was working on a replacement for the smaller models. It arrived in 1975, in the form of the new 3 series. Following BMW tradition, the new car bore a resemblance both to its highly successful predecessor and its larger four-door cousins. It looked both familiar yet new—precisely the impact BMW wanted.

The initial offerings, the 316, 318, and 320, all used the familiar old four-cylinder engine. By 1977, however, the company offered variants of the M60 six-cylinder unit in the 320 and the new 323i. They met with a mixed reception. Commentators had begun to complain about the way BMW rarely made fundamental change; instead its new models invariably seemed an evolution of the old. The policy of introducing the new model in its most mundane, small-engined guise also had an impact. BMW tended to enhance the performance of its cars toward the end of their life cycle, to an extent that made them class leaders. This attracted favorable press comment and stimulated sales of vehicles about to be replaced. In this way models such as the 2000Ti and 2002Ti or 3.0Si were always regarded as the most appealing of the range. When the new model was introduced, it would appear unexciting in contrast. Although buyers attracted by a new model would pick up sales, enthusiasts for the marque were often disappointed. They waited expectantly for the larger and more highly developed machines that would emerge in a year or two.

Clearly this pattern was no accident but part of a conscious marketing strategy to protect long-running product cycles within a climate where BMW knew it could sell

everything it could produce. Other manufacturers often introduced the high-end model first and then slowly and unobtrusively released its more mundane relations, picking up sales on the established prestige and impact of the lead model. BMW took the opposite approach, building excitement and sales with each model year so that the final year's model would sell out, creating an appetite for the company's new offering.

The public and press welcomed the 3 series in its appearance and features but were concerned that it lacked the sheer performance of the 2002Ti and Tii models. The 3 series had a slight weight penalty when compared with the outgoing 02 coupes. Responding to criticisms of the car's power, BMW shortly introduced the 323i with a claimed 143 horsepower from its six-cylinder power unit.

Whatever criticisms may be leveled at their performance in four-cylinder form, the new models did bring real improvements. Sophisticated and effective heating and ventilation provided better driver comfort. In line with industry practices, the company also made some improvement in corrosion resistance and crash protection—U.S.-spec 2002s, for example, had required rear strengthening beams to improve crash protection. Similarly, the vulnerable rear-mounted fuel tank of the 02 series gave way to a more protected underfloor location on the new car. Sound deadening

The 1977 7 series was not BMW's best styling effort and somehow never had the cachet of the big Mercedes and Jaguar models, though it was perhaps more of a driver's car than either.

This 728i is owned by Tim Hignett of L&C BMW and has never been registered or used on the road! It shows the later styling, with better aerodynamics.

was greatly improved, and there was some reduction in wind noise as a result of better side window sealing.

Once again, BMW had succeeded in producing a car that was conventional in all respects, avoided technological frontiers, and yet performed well against its competitors. It incorporated industry best practice in the design and manufacture of the cars and judged their market well. Not that the 3 series were without fault—whatever the brochures may imply, they were not particularly economical, in either four- or six-cylinder form. Initially, the handling was suspect, and the ride was not ideal. Engineers made some changes to spring rates within a few months of introduction, and the development process continued through the life of the cars—both in response to recognized weaknesses, and according to BMW's philosophy of improving its cars over time.

A longer-stroke M60 engine with K-Jetronic injection gave the 323i a healthy increase in performance over the 320. Once again it was a model that sold well, but always lacked the appeal for enthusiasts of the original 2002Tii. It was softer and less involving to drive, though in many ways a more civilized car.

The 323i had little direct competition. One cannot readily think of other moderate-size performance cars of quality with large engines. Perhaps its natural competition came in the form of large-engined rear-wheel-drive coupes from the mass manufacturers. Opel's fine Monza coupe and even Ford's V-6 Capris could challenge the BMW's performance and handling. Yet they appear cumbersome and unsophisticated in comparison. Certainly their image was no match for the BMW's. The Opel was considerably more expensive than the BMW, while the Ford was cheaper and looked it.

Real competition for the 323i came perhaps in another guise. VW, with its newly introduced Golf GTi, had produced a front-wheel-drive car that offered enthusiastic drivers real rewards. It combined sparkling performance, good build quality, and excellent chassis response. It was functional and rational in the same way as the BMW was, at about 70 percent of the cost of a 323i. It was also markedly more economical.

Of course it did not pose a direct threat within BMW's consumer base. Its obvious connection to the mundane, the economical Golf ensured that. BMW purchasers may have prided themselves on their rationality, but they were certainly conscious of the messages associated with BMW ownership.

Nevertheless VW's dominant Golf GTi may have persuaded BMW to shift its attentions away from smaller performance models and to put more performance into its larger and more expensive cars. This was a wise decision, reinforcing the marque's perceived exclusiveness and identity, at a time when the fortunes of many manufacturers were undergoing major changes.

By the early 1980s, the 3 series was due for a facelift. It came in the form of the newly designated E30 range. Minor modifications to both the 3 and 5 series involved raising the rear boot line and a range of subtle changes to make both models more appealing. Long overdue five-speed gearboxes appeared, while in 1982 a four-door version of the 3 series bodyshell was introduced.

There was even a weight reduction across the range. Many of the desirable features were part of a long options list that included things we might expect as standard, like the four doors, five-speed gearbox, and power steering. Slowly over the years the options would be incorporated into the standard specification, but BMW (like Mercedes) always operated with a large options list to inflate the already high price. Customers seemed willing to purchase enhanced specification models, and the dealerships became expert in selling upgrades like alloy wheels, sunroofs, and similar additions, all carrying large, profitable price tags.

The face-lift in the early 1980s on both the 3 and 5 series, though apparently minor, did make a real difference

A center spread from a 7 series brochure shows BMW's literate and technically orientated advertising. Note the more angular nose treatment on the early model; the aerodynamics were poor.

A new concept of motoring in the highest luxury class: The BMW 7 Series.

BMW cars are among the small international group of alternatives considered when the buyer is seeking a motor car of the highest quality. But unlike other makes in this class, which apply an almost uniform concept of passiveness and great technical sophistication to transport the motorist in as insulated and comfortable a way as possible, BMW offer the alternative of a driver-orientated, sporting and dynamic, high-performance motor car.

In the 7 Series BMWs we have used this concept to take a decisive step into the future of motoring, we have combined the classic BMW virtues with qualities which could hitherto be found only in a few exclusive luxury cars.

As cars designed specifically in contrast, the large BMWs are specially designed to provide an alternative for buyers who want maximum luxury and comfort without sluggishness and a ponderous and ostentatious image. The large BMWs are therefore made for drivers who regard a high standard of dynamism and vitality as a prerequisite for – and not a contradiction to – true exclusivity.

The new generation of large BMWs opens up new perspectives for the most demanding motorist: BMW 728, 732i, 735i, 745i.

With the introduction of the 7-Series BMWs we offer motorists a concept that fits ideally into the traffic conditions of today and, equally importantly, of tomorrow. These cars, which have been consistently improved for optimum quality, combine outstanding performance and absolute luxury to a new standard of economy and progressiveness in design. They feature many important improvements and refined parts and components: fuel injection power units optimized for maximum economy, high performance and minimum exhaust emissions, sophisticated electronic systems which create a new standard in automotive engineering, and an exemplary level of quality and all-round perfection.

to the attractiveness of the cars. Subtle changes to screen pillars and roof lines helped the proportions, while improved trim and interior fabrics enhanced the cars' quality appearance. Many of the revisions also were linked to reducing production costs and taking advantage of new production technologies.

Manufacturers like BMW who commit to long production runs have to perform a careful balancing act.

The long runs allow a full return on the tooling and development costs. On the other hand, the long runs can inhibit the adoption of new production methods and innovations. This in turn can erode competitiveness and quality. BMW seems always to have found a way through these delicate decisions and to have developed a business with accountancy and managerial systems that provided appropriate information to the decision-makers.

TURBO SUPER SALOON—THE 745i

The 745i was built by BMW in response to Stuttgart's big, new 5.0-liter S-Class, a 140-mile-per-hour express for the most hard-charging of Europe's executives. Munich claimed the moral high ground with this new 252-horsepower super-sedan, stepping back from the unseemly headlong rush toward bigger, thirstier V-8 and V-12 engines in rival Euro flagships.

Plans for its own V-12 engine had been ditched, in the wake of the fuel crisis, in favor of a turbocharged version of the familiar 3.2-liter straight six, for which superior economy was claimed but with performance exceeding 140 miles per hour.

They called it a more "socially responsible" solution and even showed pictures of the stillborn V-12 in the 7 series brochure to ram the point home.

The 745i designation derives from a formula for the displacement equivalent of a turbocharged engine. Basically, a turbo is thought to be worth a 40 percent gain in displacement, hence the 745 appellation—a 7 series, with a 3.2-liter engine boosted 40 percent to a 4.5-liter equivalent.

The waste-gated K27 KKK blower upped the torque by 30 percent, with 284 ft-lb at an impressively low 2,600 rpm. A recirculation device kept the turbine speed high even on a closed throttle, so although the boost level was low at just 0.6 bar, it was sustained from 2,000 rpm all the way to the 6,300 rpm redline. This minimized the throttle lag and vicious on/off delivery that afflicted so many early turbos—BMW's own blown 2002 being one of the worst culprits.

Naturally the canted-over big-block six was substantially altered to handle its new role. Cam profiles, timing, and fuel metering

in the injection were modified in the name of low-end torque. Valves were made of Nimonic high-pressure alloy, and the bottom end of the engine had beefed-up bearing shells with higher wear resistance. An oil cooler was considered essential because of the higher temperatures involved.

Automatic transmission was standardized on the 745i—a ZF three-speed—with a longer final drive for more relaxed cruising and a higher top speed. Bosch ABS for the vented four-wheel disc brakes became standard too. The suspension was basically that of the 735i—struts at the front, semi-trailing arms to the rear—but with the option of a sports setup comprising a reinforced anti-roll bar and beefed-up shocks. There back was self-leveling.

The car was launched in 1981 to favorable reviews, particularly in America, where such swift and stable four-door luxury sedans were something of a novelty.

It would have gone down well in the United Kingdom too, had BMW built a right-hand-drive version, but the blower would have gotten in the way of the steering column. The low volumes envisaged for the car were probably the deciding factor in keeping it left-hand drive only. It was Alpina rather than BMW that came up with a really quick, sporty 7 series for the British market in the form of the B10.

It wasn't so much the off-the-mark acceleration that made the 745 such an entertainingly quick 2-ton limousine, but its pickup beyond, say, 50 miles per hour. Punch the pedal to the floor, feel the ZF box drop into second, and feel that sweet, muscular straight six sweep the car away in a seamless rush of energy that wouldn't

In this respect they appear to have been well in advance of most other European manufacturers, who show much less skill in managing their model runs and production systems to ensure profitability.

Slowly the 3 series evolved, responding to the requirements of different markets with different combinations of engine size and specification. In the increasingly fuel- and emissions-conscious 1980s, more of the range acquired fuel injection. Injection systems themselves became more sophisticated, with Bosch L-Jetronic electronic systems taking the place of the earlier mechanical K-Jetronic system. Compression ratios fell as unleaded gasoline with lower octane ratings came to the fore in much of Europe and the United States. And in the chassis department, ABS was introduced, initially as an expensive option on the top models. Most of the changes,

begin to tail off until 130 miles per hour or more. No lag, no hesitation—and all this from an engine that was as torquey and refined as its normally aspirated cousin. With the sports suspension, the lurch and dive that afflicted lesser species of 7 series is largely eliminated, and the keen pilot could toss this big car through bends like something half its size, enjoying high-quality power steering that combined feel and feedback with decent response.

The other great thing about the 745 was that it looked just like any other E23 7 series. The shape had been about since 1977, a chunky slab-sided affair from the pen of Paul Bracq, who was also responsible for the 6 series coupe of the year before.

Good as it was, the 745i didn't win over many buyers. Sales couldn't sustain the 10-car-a-day production levels hoped for, and it was always a marginal machine in the grand scheme of BMW production.

This isn't to say that BMW let its flagship wither on the vine. From 1983 an improved version was introduced using the 3.5-liter straight six, and, more importantly, a new four-speed ZF automatic transmission with electronically switchable sport and economy modes, and a lock-up overdrive top. Officially this auto was the only 745 transmission option, but a handful of five-speed manuals were built to special order.

Power was unchanged, but torque was down slightly to 275 ft-lb. Fortunately, it was produced at a lower 2,200 rpm, making the range of usable performance rather wider so that this version felt quicker lower down the range.

You can spot one of these later 745s by its more rounded nose and bib spoiler, which reduced the barn door drag coefficient of the E23 body by 9 percent. By using a 13-degree semi-trailing arm angle, in conjunction with increased anti-squat and anti-toe geometry, the new model handled more predictably too, especially in wet conditions.

In its twilight years, BMW offered a fully loaded "Executive" 745i with all the options the busy tycoon could want, whether he or she was behind the wheel or lounging in the back. Buffalo hide covered not only the seats but also the center console and dashboard, and even the gear lever. Electric front seats were already pretty commonplace in the upmarket luxury field, but the 745 Executive came with powered rear seats, not to mention a car phone installation in the center console, rear window blinds and all the latest cruise and climate control systems.

North America's gray import industry ensured that many 745i models found their way to the States, but in Britain, where the E23 7 series rapidly went out of fashion after its demise in 1986, there was never much call for it, even as a personal import.

Ultimately, the 745 was not a refined car as we know refined cars today. In fact, even in the early 1980s, it wasn't quite in the ultimate class in terms of chassis composure. Its wheels fell heavily into potholes and crashed over bumps, and without the silent, flowing-cream delivery of a V-12 Jaguar or the effortless feel of a big V-8 Mercury, it seemed a little too aggressively sporty to its middle-aged target audience.

BMW probably realized it wasn't the answer early on and the 745 was effectively replaced by the V-12-engined car it knew it needed all along: smoother, faster, and no less economical.

Still, the 745i remains as a fascinating cul-de-sac in BMW history and easily the most covetable of E23 saloons.

Well, almost. In South Africa another kind of 745i was marketed with the M88 24-valve motorsport straight six.

BMW extended the "M" treatment to the 6 series coupe to produce the M635 in 1984. Here at last was a 6 series car that could hold its head up with the likes of the Porsche 928 and Ferrari 328GTB. This car is owned by Munich Legends, the United Kingdom-based BMW specialists.

The Motorsport straight six was a visually attractive engine and has proved reliable in service, although it is expensive to repair should it go wrong. Although it's been more than a decade since BMW produced one, these car are in high demand as usable modern classics.

like the wider wheels with lower-profile tires, combined marketing initiative with adaptation to new developments by suppliers, in line with industry trends.

By the mid-1980s the top 3 series model had grown in engine size to become the 325i, with a claimed 170 horsepower from its further-stretched engine. It was an impressive car, but by the mid-to-late 1980s the performance-car market was once again thriving. Small, hot hatchbacks like the Golf GTi and Peugeot 205GTi, (primarily in Europe and the United Kingdom) with powerful engines in small, light, front-wheel-drive shells had nurtured a more demanding public. Social attitudes throughout Europe had also changed.

Environmental awareness has grown but a consumer boom was also under way and performance models were increasingly important to all manufacturers; motorsport was an increasingly important marketing tool. Even Mercedes had been affected, introducing the curious 2.3 Cosworth-headed 190E 16-valve. Ford had found European competition and market success in 1986 with the Sierra Cosworth, which moved the performance benchmarks with its raucous turbocharged engine. By 1987 Lancia had produced the startling Integrale, with four-wheel drive and a massively powerful turbo engine shoehorned into a bodyshell and floorpan that owed their origins many years earlier to the humble Fiat Strada. Audi had also turned its image around and attracted great attention with the Quattro Turbo.

In comparison to these models BMW's 325 was tame and flabby. Further up the range, of course, the impressive M535 sedans combined performance and luxury, while highly developed 635 coupes were finding surprising success on the track. But there was clearly sales and market prestige to be gained from including a production "homologation special" in the range.

The result was the M3, which in its original form is perhaps one of the most exciting road cars of the period. The M3 abandoned the M60 six-cylinder engine in favor of a 2.3 liter naturally aspirated four-cylinder unit, whose origins can be traced back to the original BMW M12 Formula 2 engines. Going back further, the same engine derives from the original slant four found in the first BMW *neu classe* sedans. Fitted with a modern 16-valve double overhead cam (DOHC) head, the engine was a powerful throaty unit that in competition form made an unforgettable sound. In road-going guise, it lost some of its bark but remained a highly strung unit with sensational response and the ability to rev and rev. The body was considerably modified in ways not all of which are immediately apparent. Most obvious are the flared wheel arches designed to cover the wider rims. Less noticeable are the subtle changes to the rear window angle. A plastic frame is used to alter the rake and improve the aerodynamics in conjunction with a raised boot line and rear spoiler.

The M3 offered few concessions to refinement, with vibration and resonance periods at the most awkward points for everyday road use. Unlike most of its turbo competitors, this was not a car with a docile side. The chassis likewise lost the compliance and softness that had characterized—some say marred—all the other 3 series models. Instead it acquired a dart-like precision. Higher-geared steering, along with firmer damping and higher spring rates, transformed the responses of the car to match its new purpose. In its original form, the M3 quickly acquired the title of the ultimate driver's car. It was both powerful and responsive, but the driver had to be continually involved and was not insulated from the vehicle's behavior by traction control or four-wheel drive, as in the new generation of supercars. Perhaps best of all, the naturally aspirated engine had the instant response and progressive delivery of power that turbo cars of the period lacked.

The Americans didn't get their version of the Motorsport 6 series until 1986, and with a lower compression ratio it developed a less-impressive 256 horsepower at 6,500 rpm.

This is a late-model "Highline" M635CSi for the British market with color-coded bumpers, leather trim, electric seats, and air conditioning. It is owned by Tim Hignett of L&C BMW.

BMW's art car tradition continued with this 635CSi painted by Robert Rauschenberg and owned by BMW Mobile Tradition in Munich. Unlike previous art cars, it was a standard production model, not a racing car.

As always with BMW, the engineering underlying the creation of even the best of its cars was thoroughly conventional. Any one of innumerable manufacturers' engineering departments could have, given the guidelines, devised a similar vehicle. The M3 was most akin in its responses and driver rewards to a road-going Ford Escort works rally car of the 1970s. Despite, or because of, its competition orientation, the M3 was a sales success. It sold well throughout Europe during the car's production run, from 1985 to 1991, in the original body shape. In total over 17,000 of the E30 series M3s were produced with exports going to all BMW's key markets.

Each year additional components were homologated to maintain the M3's competitiveness in motorsport. The resulting 500-odd evolution road cars came to be particularly sought after. In 1987 minor bodywork changes to improve aerodynamics gave rise to the Evolution 1. By the next year new cams and various other changes boosted power to 220 horsepower. By the end of 1989 a further Evolution model had emerged with an enlarged 2.5-liter engine with a claimed 238 horsepower at 7,000 rpm.

Alongside the M3 Evolution models generated by the motorsport homologation procedures, BMW produced various special editions to respond to market opportunity. The cabriolet body style could also be had in M3 form. These variants can perhaps be seen as marketing confections of the worst kind. They involved taking the M3 and loading it with the features of the more luxurious models and more dubious add-on spoilers. It is a paradox not confined to BMW. Manufacturers develop a model for sporting use, stripping it of weight and luxury features. Its sporting success and image attracts customers who are anxious to buy the newest, most talked-about model. So commercial logic dictates that the manufacturers then start loading the model with the very features that they had originally discarded. In the M3's case most of those buying the convertibles and leather-trimmed versions would probably have been happier with a more restful and forgiving 325i with its silky smooth engine and more docile nature.

Given its character the M3 has always appealed to enthusiasts but it is more difficult to assess its impact on BMW as a company. Without the M3, BMW would

A new E30 3 series made its debut in 1983 and retained a styling link with the previous model, but there were many detail changes, mostly aimed at refining the chassis for improved ride and more predictable handling. Initially the engine range was much the same. A four-door version, the first for BMW's smallest car, came in 1983.

perhaps have had difficulty maintaining its sporting image. Clearly BMW's major investment in European touring-car racing in the late 1980s and early 1990s reflected the company's perception that motorsport exposure had real benefit for sales. Though BMW was successful in the British Touring Car series with the M3, this was only a pale shadow of its involvement in Germany and the rest of Europe, where its sedan racing profile was much higher. The actual results were perhaps of less importance than maintaining the perception that BMW was a marque with a sporting character. The M3 also influenced the way the rest of the 3 series range was perceived. At a time when the 3 series was not really in a class-leading position in terms of performance and handling, and the range was open to criticism, the M3 produced the positive headlines the company needed.

The New-Generation Coupes

The CS series coupes were successful both commercially and in terms of their contribution to BMW's growth as a leading prestige carmaker. Expensive, stylish, and with acceptable performance, they sold well in both the United States and Europe. Despite their weight and grand touring orientation, they were also

transformed into successful racecars. In short they were a difficult act to follow.

Yet by 1976 BMW was well advanced in its plan to replace the existing large-sedan range with the new Paul Bracq–designed 7 series cars. Accompanying this change was to be the new 6 series coupes, sharing many of their features and the design philosophy of the 7 series, but based on the shorter 5 series floorpan. As always with BMW, the first model to be introduced left lots of room for obvious development, yet was sufficiently attractive in its own right to capture attention. The 630 with carbureted 3.0-liter engine appeared in 1976, to be replaced a year later by the fuel-injected 628. By 1979 the flagship 635Csi had arrived. Mechanically they differed little from top-end 5 and 7 series cars.

Heavy, expensive, and—once the range was under way—beautifully built, they provided a stylish alternative to the luxury sedans for those for whom cost was of little consequence. Most of the early models were sold as automatics, and their weight was such that performance and handling was little different from their sedan parents. The initial production run had bodies built by Karmann, and some of these had serious quality control problems. By August 1977, production was moved in-house to Dingolfing, with Karmann at Osnabruck supplying the body only in bare shell form for subsequent assembly. Around 6,000 per year were built in the late 1970s and, as always with BMW, pricing left good margins even for such an apparently complex and sophisticated car. Despite its apparent complexity, it had been designed for ease of production, and most of the components were common to other vehicles in the range. In this way development costs were limited, and the risk of teething troubles and warranty claims reduced.

In terms of styling, the 6 series cars were perhaps hampered by a relatively short wheelbase and large front and rear overhang. To an extent they lacked the styling distinction of the earlier CS coupes. Nevertheless a quarter of a century after their introduction they still appear pleasing and modern. Their position in the market reflected BMW's aspirations. On the one hand, they were certainly able to rival the Mercedes coupes in their long-distance cruising abilities. Unlike the Mercedes

and Jaguar XJS, which tended invariably to come in automatic form, the BMWs were available with a choice of two manual gearboxes alongside the automatic option. Either an overdrive five-speed or a close-ratio box could be specified, to reflect the concerns of the owner. Obviously the close-ratio box offered drivers greater involvement, while the overdrive option enhanced the car's refinement in long-distance use. By 1984 the automatic was greatly improved with the addition of an electronically controlled "sport" option. Though common today, BMW was one of the first manufacturers to offer this feature on their cars, and in the case of their large-engined sedans and coupes it was a very worthwhile innovation.

Six series handling was more entertaining than either the Jaguar's or the Mercedes' and they had a rather more discreet image that suited BMW's target market. Admittedly the 635CSi sprouted a small spoiler and some striping in the early years of its production, but by the mid-1980s most were being produced in restrained

Baur continued with the Targa-topped version of the new 3 series, even after BMW introduced its own full convertible version in 1986, although sales were down to a trickle.

colors, and some had a discreet dechromed appearance that suited the cars well. Careful development allowed them to achieve success in European touring-car racing, where they were victorious in 1981, 1983, and 1986.

Once again these were competent rather than innovative cars. For their time they brought a daunting array of electronic gadgetry, but BMW's relationship with its suppliers tended to ensure that it continued to work. The car's features performed with smoothness and grace, and they appeared—as indeed they were—built to last. Occasional camshaft lubrication and cylinder head porosity problems are the only things documented as problems associated with the model. Models from late 1980 acquired a much more sophisticated Bosch digital engine management systems that improved fuel consumption and drivability, while subtle changes in trim and equipment made the more recent cars more appealing. Early examples with cloth, rather than the optional leather interior, came to look quite dull and uninspiring as they aged. On balance, the 6 series cars found a safe niche in the marketplace and enhanced the BMW name, but did not really become benchmarks against which other manufacturers' offerings were measured. Over 50,000 of the 635 model were produced with smaller numbers of the other variants.

Toward the end of their production life the 6 series range included a new ultrahigh-performance model. Introduced in 1983, the M635 used the fabulous M series 24-valve twin-cam engine, which moved the performance of the big coupe well into the supercar league. The M635 is perhaps the most sought-after modern BMW coupe and provides the kind of raw exhilaration that comes from a large, naturally aspirated engine in a rear-wheel-drive chassis. The M6, as it later came to be known, retained all the flexibility and luxury of the 12-valve cars, but now had the performance to match the Porsche 928, which BMW saw as a serious threat to its market position.

It is, of course, doubtful if buyers of cars such as the 928 and the 635 would notice differences of a few tenths of a second in performance in cars which, by any standards, are awesomely fast. What does matter though to manufacturers such as BMW, and their customers, is the perception that they are producing the best. Pride in ownership can quickly be eroded once it is generally known that the product you possess isn't quite the fastest, most modern, or most coveted. Given BMW's price tags, its flagship models have to outshine their competitors. By the late 1980s the long-running 6 series, even in M6 guise, had become a familiar part of the

The 1985–1991 M3 was a homologation special built to take on Mercedes in Group A racing, for which 5,000 examples had to be built. It was the most exciting small BMW since the 2002 Turbo. The body was remodeled with 20 additional panels. This is an "Evo III" with a slightly different spoiler treatment and a second blade to the rear spoiler.

The last and most exciting M3 was the Evolution III, with a bigger 2.5-liter engine producing 238 horsepower at 7,000 rpm—giving a top speed of 152 miles per hour and 0–60 in 6.5 seconds. Front and rear spoilers were adjustable. Wheel arches were expanded to accept wider racing rubber, and the front suspension was lowered.

motoring landscape. Respected and admired, it no longer had the image to grab the headlines.

By the late 1980s BMW had already successfully introduced its new 7 series. The new big sedans appeared less cumbersome than their rather slab-sided predecessors and received a warm welcome. A new coupe was overdue, yet when it arrived in the form of the 850i, with new alloy V-12 5.0-liter engine and sophisticated electronics, even ardent BMW fans among the corps of motoring journalists still voiced a few reservations.

Impressive though the car undoubtedly was, the appearance, to some eyes, lacked the delicacy and elegance that BMW had instinctively achieved in other models. On the road it performed effortlessly and cocooned driver and passengers in comfort and safety, yet somehow it failed to inspire and excite. Clearly BMW had chosen to move the model even further upmarket with levels of refinement that take away some of the excitement you might expect to accompany such high levels of performance.

By the late 1980s, manufacturers had moved into a race to achieve headline-grabbing performance figures. The 850, despite its great weight, was a formidable performer but this was a period when outright maximum speeds were, once again, being used to convey marketing messages. The 850 didn't always come out at the top of the supercar performance league.

There were other factors at work that would undermine the 850, yet benefit the new generation of sedans, such as the impressive M5. By the late 1980s supercars were becoming so large, heavy, and sophisticated that they also seemed pointless. Manufacturers were using new lightweight materials and sophisticated design processes to eliminate excess weight, yet the result was not light cars but cars that were just not quite as grotesquely heavy as they might otherwise have been. As top speeds grew, and engine power increased, tire size and tire noise grew, requiring further chassis sophistication. Electronic ABS systems and traction control were required to tame cars that produced massive power, yet they in turn reduced the level of driver involvement.

All these developments could be incorporated as easily into a sedan shell as they could into a coupe. The organic connection between a car's body configuration and its dynamic qualities had been severed to some extent many years earlier. By the late 1980s it had become almost easier to manufacturer a sedan with extraordinary performance that would reward with driving pleasure while being both practical and usable, than it was to manufacturer a coupe with all its limitations.

Coupes were no longer lighter than their sedan brethren. It was far from certain that an appealing two-door

The M3 was an instant hit in the late 1980s, recapturing the aggression and rawness of cars like the CSL and 2002 Turbo.

coupe bodyshell could be made as stiff as a carefully designed four-door sedan shell because of the coupe's proportions and need for thin screen pillars. Similarly, engine locations no longer gave them the enhanced turn-in and quickness of response that marked the sports car of an earlier era. At one time coupes would have engines set further back in the chassis than the typical sedan.

By the late 1980s the positioning of air conditioning equipment and ventilation ducts were likely to determine engine positioning more effectively than any consideration of dynamic qualities. In short, modern developments constrain the coupe more than the sedan.

Of course, BMW continued with the 8 series, introducing the more potent 850CSi in October 1992 in

THE CULT OF THE M5

Q-car challengers have come and gone since the original BMW M5's 1985 launch—remember the Lotus Carlton and the Mercury 500E?—but as the ultimate in understated four-door hotshots, the E28 remains one of the best of the lot.

It is not merely the bald facts of its supercar-slaying urge—a rev-limited 154 miles per hour and 0–60 in 6.3 seconds—that were so stunning at the time but the docility, the smooth unflustered maturity of its gut-wrenching delivery. The in-gear acceleration figures reveal a car built for the realities of the autobahn, where supersharp throttle response and a properly thought-out set of gear ratios count for everything. With only discreet "M5" badges, fat tires, and some subtle spoilers to give it away, the M5 could run comfortably with lesser species of V-8 Ferrari and nonturboed Porsche 911s, return 20 miles per gallon if you weren't trying too hard, and cruise all day at 130 miles per hour in air-conditioned, six-speaker luxury.

Throw in terrific handling, a practical and well-appointed bodyshell, and the enduring appeal of BMW build quality, and you can see why many critics were moved to describe the M5 as one of the best sedans money could buy.

Launched at the beginning of 1985, the M5 is not to be confused with the much tamer, single-cam M535 that uses the same prosaic four-door shell dating back to the mid-1970s. This car was merely fast by virtue of squeezing the biggest single-cam six into a midrange body; the concept lacked finesse, and the handling tended to disappoint.

The most important component in the M5 was BMW's classic 24-valve twin-cam straight six, first seen in the M1 and then, in the mid-1980s, the M635 coupe. It revved higher and punched much

harder than the single-cam engine, delivering 286 horsepower at 6,500 rpm with 251 ft-lb of torque at 4,500 rpm.

Canted 30 degrees, the basic iron block was from the mid-engined M1 (without the dry sump) but the M5 ran a higher compression ratio and second-generation Bosch ML-Jetronic injection and engine management for a whisper quiet, smooth idle. Under the crackle-black cam cover was single-row chain drive for the cams and Malhe pistons, but the alternator and fan coupling are shared with the stock car. The five-speed gearbox (there was no automatic option) was specially made by Getrag to BMW's design, and by tweaking the suspension, the Motorsport department made the M5's handling much more special. Patented "Track link" rear suspension banished lift-off oversteer, and shorter progressive rate springs and gas pressure struts cut out body roll without spoiling the ride. Massive Pirelli P700 tires on special 16-inch alloys conferred impressive grip, certainly superior to the TRX-shod M635 of slightly earlier vintage.

The M5—unlike the M3 and M635—was hand-assembled in a Munich suburb by a team of 75 specially trained BMW Motorsport engineers. Each car took a week to build, and production was limited to around 2,000 a year. BMW even invited M5 owners to come and watch their car being built on the production line.

The total production run was something under 5,000; 1,235 of those went to the United States, even though BMW originally claimed it would only send 500. Aggrieved owners, angry at the dilution of their exclusivity, organized a lawsuit claiming false advertising, but the case was settled when every American M5 owner was given a credit toward a new BMW.

BMW settled on a four-cylinder engine, rather than a six, for the M3 as it was a lighter, stronger option and developed 200 horsepower from 2.3 liters. The block was related to the 1.5-liter engine developed for the New Class in 1961. It featured double overhead cams, 16 valves, and the latest fuel injection technology.

order to stay in the horsepower race. A projected M8, with even more power from a quad-cam 48-valve version of the V-12, never got beyond the prototype stage. BMW management was reputed to have vetoed the development. According to Wolfgang Rietzel, head of BMW research and development, BMW was "just not interested in putting our name to cars like these any more." The mood of the times had changed, and BMW's position in the market required a more subtle management of the performance image than would result from bespoilered, production-derived supercars.

Instead, the 8 series was extended to include the 840Ci coupe with a V-8 engine and a lower price. It was a logical move, as the V-8 unit offered good performance and refinement and sales of the V-12 had been sluggish. BMW in the early 1990s was a very different company from the BMW that existed when the 6 series was first introduced in the mid-1970s. It was now the acknowledged quality performance carmaker. It was the benchmark against which other manufacturers measured themselves. In the market it had a virtually unrivaled image. As a business it now produced very much greater volumes compared to the 1970s, and had margins that other manufacturers envied. Within this framework, the big 8 series coupes had played a part and contributed to the company's fortunes. BMW's success, however, was

Inside, the Evo Sport had a new steering wheel with suede trim and new anthracite-striped Motorsport seats, but in the name of lightness it did without luxury items like electric windows and air conditioning.

Eight hundred M3 cabriolets were produced, hand-built by BMW's Motorsport staff with the full specification of the closed car. They continued in production until 1991. Unlike the standard open-topped 3 series, the top was electrically operated.

based on the high-volume 3 and 5 series cars. The future of the 8 series was of less concern; the days of the large luxurious coupe were numbered.

The 7 Series Sedans: Completing the Range

BMW's 7 series top-of-the-range sedans emerged in May 1977. Initially in 2.8-liter form the cars were aimed straight at the Mercedes S class models. Once again BMW avoided technical novelty and produced a car with tried and tested components but engineered to produce greater driver appeal than the rather softer and less agile large Mercedes. In its day it was regarded as impressive both in terms of appearance and performance. As the years have passed, it perhaps has lost something of its appeal. In particular its rather slab-sided appearance makes it less elegant than some other BMW models. On the other hand, there is no doubting these were finely engineered cars with ride, handling, and performance well up to the best standards of the day.

BMW used a variety of engines ranging from the thirsty carbureted units in the 728 and 730s—sometimes in surprisingly basic form with manual windows

and four-speed manual gearboxes—through more potent and better-equipped injected 3.2- and 3.5-liter versions introduced in 1979. From 1982, the range got a series of subtle but important improvements. Minor restyling of the nose gave the car a better appearance, while a more modern four-speed automatic gearbox was a major benefit, as the original three-speed unit undermined the appeal of the car to enthusiastic drivers. Welcome modifications to the rear suspension also aided handling while a series of minor equipment and trim changes ensured the car kept abreast of the its competitors at the top of the luxury market. For their size, the injected 7 series cars were reasonably economical and outstandingly robust.

Rarest of all was the misleadingly named 745i. Not a 4.5-liter derivative, but a turbocharged version of the 732i, this big sedan offered startling performance for a car of its size. The turbo installation meant it was only available in left-hand-drive form, as the large intercooled KKK turbo would interfere with a right-hand-drive steering column. By all accounts, the installation worked well but as with all turbo installations of the time, there was some turbo lag. Although the ultimate power was increased, the most impressive feature of the turbocharged unit was its torque curve. Massive torque was spread right across the rev range, complementing the unit's noted willingness to rev and producing a car with outstanding performance.

On the other hand, these figures can mislead about the experience of driving the car. It may have been able to produce massive torque at low rpm but as with most early turbo cars, the lowered compression meant that initial low-speed, off-boost, response was not that impressive. Linked to a three-speed auto transmission in the original version, the car was well suited to high-speed cruising but perhaps not as enjoyable as you might expect on a winding road. Virtually every 745i was produced in automatic form, which may suggest BMW was worried about the torque capacity of some parts of the manual drivetrain. Alternatively, it may just reflect BMW's perception that the car was more an autobahn cruiser than a sports car. Perhaps surprisingly given its torque curve, the 745i was one of the models most improved by the switch to the four-speed automatic. Of course BMW had envisaged that its top-of-the-range model would be V-12 powered, but it was not until the second-generation 7 series saw the light of day that the V-12 engine finally emerged. Rumor has it that BMW halted V-12 development when gas prices increased in the mid-1970s, because the engine was obviously going to seem an extravagance.

This M3 art car was produced by Australian artist Ken Done. The inspiration for the design was Australian fish.

The new 7 series was announced in 1985 and by 1988 had a new flagship in the form of the V-12-engined 750iL. It was a fine car, but seemed somehow superfluous, especially after BMW introduced its new V-8 engines at the beginning of the 1990s. They make an astonishingly cheap buy secondhand.

BMW's big V-12-engined cars have always been rather disappointing and curiously irrelevant. They have never captured buyers' hearts like the biggest S-Class Mercedes models.

For much of the cars' history, BMW made the 3, 5, and 7 series models roughly in the proportions of 65, 25, and 20 percent of production though these proportions vary toward the end of each model cycle. By the late 1980s, though, the 5 series came to increasing prominence and the numbers of 7 series also increased with the arrival of the new second-generation car. The new model, introduced in 1986, somehow had an elegance and proportion that the earlier Paul Braque–designed 7 series lacked. Mechanically it remained conventional.

Perhaps the biggest change was from the self-conscious electronic componentry in the first 7 series to more integrated systems in the new car. Sophisticated ABS, climate control, and engine management systems were developed for the car, offering a new refinement and poise.

As with the early car, a range of engine sizes were offered, though in this case they stretched from the entry level, but very competent, 728, up to the new 12-cylinder 750i, available in both standard and long-wheelbase body versions.

Even the big 5.0-liter V-12 sold well, with nearly 20,000 produced in its first year of production. It outsold Mercedes' comparable S class models of the time and was generally well received. The all-alloy V-12 was an impressive, unit but some motoring journalists found it less refined than the rather thirstier and older Jaguar V-12. Some years later, with the introduction in 1993 of the superb alloy 4.0-liter V-8, the complex V-12 seemed to offer little benefit. The V-8 used less fuel, produced similar performance and offered similar, if not better, standards of refinement. In part this was simply a measure of the pace of development. It is also important to remember that an engine's perceived refinement can have as much or more to do with its mountings and the arrangement of its ancillaries as with any characteristic of the engine itself. Moreover, at the time of the V-8's introduction the V-12 had already been under development for some considerable number of years so it was not at the leading edge of technology.

The 850 replaced the 6 series in 1989. It was fast and capable and technically complex but somehow failed to capture drivers' imaginations in the way the previous generation of cars had.

The styling quickly became
dated and before long there
was a feeling even BMW was
embarrassed by the car.
Again the V-12 engine was
a disappointment; critics felt
the V-8-engined 840 was
the better drive.

CHAPTER 6

PROFILE RAISERS: BMW's SMALL VOLUME SPORTS AND SUPER-SPORTS CARS M1, Z1, Z8

Previous page: the M1, styled by Ital Design and partially developed by Lamborghini, is one of the most collectable of all BMWs. It was BMW's first and to date only mid-engined supercar, using the 24-valve straight six in its first road-car installation—although there had been plans to use the still secret V-12.

The M1's style, though less flamboyant than many Italian supercars, has perhaps aged rather better.

In addition to its mainstream production, BMW has always produced some cars that don't quite seem to fit into the scheme of things. We have mentioned already the classic 328 and the 507. Though produced in small numbers they had a lasting influence on the image of the marque. There were also prototypes of various kinds that feature in the histories of the marque and exert a fascination over enthusiasts as tantalizing images of what might have been. The little two-cylinder Topolino-like car of the early 1940s, the ill-fated pre-war 335, and the large 505 with its Mercedes-like body all spring to mind. As an upmarket manufacturer,

BMW also attracted the attention of the coach builders. In the early days Autenreith, in particular, produced some elegant bodies on BMW chassis and Bertone, Grabber, and others all produced various BMW-based designs. In this respect BMW was no different from many other manufacturers.

The straight-six engine was mounted north-south in the space frame chassis Lamborghini had developed. The fiberglass bodywork was unstressed.

The interior of the car was finished to conventional BMW quality standards and featured much of the same instrumentation and switchgear.

A mid-engined curiosity, the M1 was built to give BMW a presence in Group 4 racing after the demise of the CSL coupes, but took so long to develop that it was out of date by the time it was ready to race. The road version was exotic and satisfying.

If anything, BMW tended to involve outside talent less than other companies, producing some of its most successful models with an in-house design team working from a carefully established design tradition within the company. Designers like Count Albrecht Goertz and Paul Bracq received their due credit in the company but perhaps the strength of BMW's design excellence lay in its teamwork and collective transmission of design values and approaches, rather than the guiding hand of a single star designer.

Where BMW did depart from the practices of its competitors was in the way it brought to production small numbers of vehicles that other manufacturers would have left as design studies. The Ml and the Z1 fall into this category. The mid-engined M1, of course, was designed as a vehicle for motorsport use. With BMW unable to build the necessary numbers for homologation in the desired time scale, the M1 featured in its own high-profile Procar race series that accompanied the 1980–1981 Grand Prix season. In terms of publicity,

BMW produced 8,012 Z1 roadsters between 1986 and 1991. The car was a test bed for new suspension technology and also a precursor to the Z3, which would emerge in 1996.

this was effective but the M1 was a project that always had a sense of unreality about it.

The motivation for the M1 came from racing and a new set of regulations, specifically the Group Five Silhouette formula of 1976, where BMW's aging CSL, even with twin turbos and a floorpan-frying 800 horsepower, was coming up short against Porsche's all-conquering 935.

To regain lost face, BMW needed a mid-engined chassis worthy of its magnificent twin-cam 3.5-liter straight six: 400 copies would have to be built over a two-year period to qualify for the formula.

There was no room for such low-volume indulgence at Munich, so BMW's Motorsport Department, headed by Jochen Neerpasch, went to Lamborghini, armed with plans for project E26: a square tubular steel–chassised coupe with a dry-sumped 3.5-liter straight-six engine, sitting in-line and well down in the chassis behind the cockpit. Schemed around the latest Pirelli P7 rubber, the underpinnings—attributed to

Like the M1, the Z1 was more of a headline grabber than a serious production car, with its silly doors. It proved a good engineering test bed for future models and is already a collector's item.

The body was made of 15 or so plastic sections fixed to a fully galvanized steel monocoque. BMW claimed the panels could be removed in half an hour.

The Z1 was one of the first cars to have high-intensity headlamps. The body design was an aerodynamic wedge using ground effect technology for negative lift front and rear.

Lamborghini chassis wizard Dallara—were to be state of the art rather than radical: unequal length coil and wishbone suspension—with antidive/squat geometry—at each corner, meaty alloy hub carriers, huge vented disc brakes (inboard at the rear), and rack steering, with five-speed ZF transaxle to put the power down on the road. The slotted alloys were 8-inchers at the rear, 7 at the front.

The M1—"M" stood for Motorsport—was to be a first road-car outing for BMW's superb M88 twin-cam straight six, based though it was on an earlier generation of single-cam sixes dating from 1968.

In turbo group-five form it would give up to 700 horsepower, but for the road BMW deemed 277 horsepower enough, peaking at 6,500 rpm—400 rpm short of the cutout—with maximum torque of 239 ft-lb at 5,000 rpm. Only the cast-iron bottom end came off the regular BMW production line, shared with the top-line 6 series coupes. Unlike the canted-over single-cam engine the twin-cam sat upright, keeping the center of gravity low and the elegant crafted exhaust headers well clear of the head to aid cooling.

Under the handsome ribbed covers, emblazoned with the BMW Motorsport script, the M88 had a unique 24-valve twin-cam head with chain drive, a pukka forged alloy crank, and longer connecting rods. It breathed through a Kugelfischer-Bosch Indirect Injection with electronic ignition by Marelli.

Working closely with BMW Motorsport, it was up to Lamborghini to sort out the details, build the prototypes and, eventually, assemble the 400 roadcars required for homologation at the rate of two a week

Styling too was left to the Italians: Giugiaro's Ital Design was contracted to shape the body, taking inspiration from Paul Bracqs' 1972 BMW Turbo, a flamboyant gull-winged showcase for Munich's passive safety ideas constructed by Michelotti.

It wasn't long before the problems started. Prototypes were seen being tested around Sant Agata in 1977, but by then Lamborghini was in deep financial trouble—and the M1 looked like it might become a casualty. Lamborghini's government funding ran out and delay after

The door disappeared into the deep sills at the touch of a button. It wasn't the easiest car in the world to get in and out of, but the sills offered excellent side impact protection.

delay pushed the timetable back still further until, eventually, in frustration, BMW snatched the M1 project back in April 1978. By that time, seven prototypes had been built but BMW decided to transfer final production to Baur in Stuttgart. Ital Design would continue to supply the raw bodies, and Marchesi of Modena the heavy space frame chassis, riveted and bonded to the shell. BMW, taking no chances this time, did all the final testing.

That wasn't the end of the M1's birth pains. Formally launched late in 1978, it immediately fell foul of new Group Five regulations that were its *raison d'être*. The revised rules said that 400 cars had to have been sold to the public before a racing version could be used in anger.

Production delays meant that it was not homologated until 1981, by which time GT racing had moved on and the M1 no longer had the potential to be competitive.

The Procar series likewise was a curiosity, with the first five Grand Prix–qualifying drivers being contractually required to participate in the Procar race. This agreement between Bernie Ecclestone and BMW caused some disquiet at Ferrari and some other teams. The series went ahead in deference to the commercial benefits for both Ecclestone's Formula One Constructors Association and BMW. Those who saw the series remembered it as lively and exciting racing. Later March developed a turbocharged version with extensive modifications to

The engine came from the 325i but the handling of the Z1 was so good, it could easily have handled a lot more power. L&C BMW owns this example, one of the few imported into the United Kingdom.

The Z3 was a more mainstream attempt to produce a sporty two-seater BMW roadster. It has been less warmly received by the critics than it has by the buying public. The first four-cylinder cars were weedy, the 2.8 straight six rather better, but the car that has really given the model some credibility is the M roadster, powered by BMW's familiar Motorsport straight six, as found in the post-1993 M3.

produce aerodynamic downforce. That model raced successfully in the International Motor Sports Association (IMSA) Camel GTO category in the Unites States and did no harm to BMW's reputation. Nevertheless, some sources suggest that the Ml saga played a part in ensuring the departure of Jochen Neerspach—the head of BMW Motorsport, who had fathered the Ml project—in the early 1980s.

Part of the Ml's problem stems from the decision to contract with Lamborghini at the wrong time, and part can be accounted for by changing conditions in motorsport. Further, because of BMW's existing production commitments, the project was never integrated into the company's mainstream work. After all, this was a time when BMW was selling all the cars it could produce and was expanding in markets throughout the world. Nevertheless, BMW always found it useful to have a partly productionized exotic car available to attract headlines, speculation, and attention. These exotica performed something of the function of the 328 and 507 in shaping

DRIVING THE M1

If the M1 racer was never much more than a promising also-ran, the road car was always top-drawer material, one of the best.

For the price of two top-flight 6 series coupes, you got a super car that wasn't just fast (M1s were independently clocked at 161 miles per hour) but comfortable, refined, surprisingly frugal, and beautifully built.

If it conceded a little to the Italians in glamour—the stillborn V-12 engine that had originally been mooted would no doubt have raised its profile—it outpointed them all the way when it came to practicality. Few who bought road-going M1s actually drove them to work year-round. Point is, if they had wanted to they could have.

Despite its enduring crowd-pleasing ability almost two decades on, professional style pundits still don't rate the M1 as master-class Giugiaro. It looks hunched and power-packed, but somehow almost plain in the shadow of organically muscular cars like the Miura. There's an air of the pulled-punch about its folded-edge design, indecision in the side window line that denies it the presence of a Boxer, the gravitas of a Countach, or even the originality of the turbo show car. Still, who knows? Perhaps a plainer, more functional look than its flamboyant Latin contemporaries was an intentional part of the concept.

If only more Italian exotics had a cabin as well thought out and screwed together as this BMW's. Switchgear and dials came from the 6 series, so everything clicked home with impeccable precision, just like any other BMW. The tasteful, six-dial hooded instrument cluster was a model of functional clarity, the Recaro seats—short on backrest adjustment—were more comfortable than they first appeared, cupping back and buttocks firmly. Wheel arch intrusion set the pedals mildly askew, but you could adjust that three-spoke wheel for reach, so most people should be able to get comfortable in the M1, though headroom wasn't in abundance. There was a feeling of width but the ambience was somber—all subdued monochromes, the emphasis on function rather than style, with high-class leather on the outer bolsters of the seats, and gray cloth in the center to aid lateral grip.

The functional emphasis didn't mean the M1 was sparsely equipped. There were electric windows, a dual-control heating and ventilation system, and big remote-control outer door mirrors to aid your rear view, restricted on the M1 because of the slats on the rear window and the buttresses that sweep down either side of the engine lid. Luggage, along with a space-saver spare, lived in a compartment just aft of the engine. Radiator, brake servos, and the black-box brain for the injection were in the nose.

Starting the M1 from stone cold held no horrors. Injection enriched the mixture so the straight six, inches from your skull hidden under a cover and behind a pane of glass, caught first turn. Only pulling away in first hinted at the racer in the M1's genetic make-up. A long, 50-mile-per-hour bottom gear and snappy take-up of the hefty-ish twin-plate clutch make getaways ragged at first, but you soon learn to slip it a little and accept the embarrassing snarl of wasted revs.

the image of the marque with little cost. About 450 M1 cars were produced, of which 50 were pure racing machines and the rest fully equipped road cars.

Another curiosity was the Z1. Appearing originally in prototype form, as a product of BMW's advanced engineering M Technic division, it found its way into limited production in 1988. The Z1 generated a large number of column inches in the motoring and style press and once again performed the function of linking BMW with technological advance. The construction, in which plastic outer body panels were fixed to a galvanized steel chassis with a molded floor, attracted the bulk of the attention. Press photographs displaying the "unclothed" structure were used to great effect to imply something unique about the construction. Careful marketing meant it received little serious examination but was carried along by association with innovation and untested claims. Much talk of recycling, ready accident repair, and novel materials perhaps disguised the fact that neither the concept, nor the materials, nor their usage was that novel.

That's not to say the straight six was peaky or nervous: once you're rolling it slugged away cleanly from 1,000 revs, strongly from as little as 2,000 rpm even in the 131-mile per hour fourth gear.

Making full use of the gears, off-the-line performance was a little shy of the gut-wrenching punch of top-flight supercars—Boxers and Countachs, higher in horsepower, were always quicker through the gears—but was still strong and rapid enough to humble the most aggressive of hotshot tin-box moderns.

With a light flywheel, the revs shut down as quickly as they surge, so you had to be decisive with the ZF gear change, its dogleg first unfashionable even in the late 1970s, to counter jerky balking.

Meaty and metallic in quality, if not perfect in definition, its ratios were spaced to make the most of the M1's silken delivery. You'd hit the legal limit in second, almost 100 in third, the bark hardening in aggression to a full-bodied wail as the power kept steaming in, lesser cars receding ever more rapidly in the wide rearview mirror. Smooth and sweet though it is, this thoroughbred six didn't have the inexorable, turbine rev-forever quality of a good four-cam V-12, but feels as if it would pull hard like a racer all the way to its fifth gear maximum.

As you'd expect, the M1's manners were impeccable. Long fast curves were barely acknowledged, narrower more demanding B-roads, twisty and undulating, swept aside with effortless speed, total authority.

Fine steering, never truly heavy, wriggled gently with communication, low-speed understeering stodge, and heft peeling away in layers as the speed builds to give faithful turn-in bite. Fast cornering produced no noticeable roll, just neutral poise, a feeling of balance and utterly faithful predictability. With those gumball P7s biting hard, the M1 was happy to let the novice glimpse the outer limits without enticing him or her over the edge. With no sharp edges to the delivery of power, no tricks to admonish a lifted foot midcorner—or even a nervously nudged brake pedal—there is a gentle feel about the M1 that was just the right side of sanitized nannying.

There are plenty of merely fast, sharp-handling cars of course. The M1's most surprising, surpassing qualities come to light while it is about more mundane everyday business.

On motorways, cruising at three-figures, the air stream slipped quietly around the M1's well-sealed cabin. Engine cacophony, urgently aggressive under load, slipped into the background. The fat rubber slapped loud on cats' eyes (fluorescent raised studs that mark out the center of the roads in the United Kingdom) but, uncharacteristically for a German car, road noise—roar— was well suppressed.

What's more, the M1 had the well-rounded ride of a good family sedan, smothering potholes and flattening bumps like an executive express. No mid-engined upper echelon supercar rode so well before; has any since?

This polished sophistication is at the heart of the M1's appeal. Disparate and convoluted as its cross-Europe design and manufacture had been, the values and the quality behind this unfulfilled racer were always pure Munich. Refined and forgiving, not given to moments of fickle temperament that are the darker side of the super car myth, it bridged the gap between yesterday's dinosaur heavyweights and today's versatile sedan-shaped supercars.

The M roadster featured fat arches and special Motorsport alloy wheels that were wider at the back than at the front. The brakes are from the M3 and the roadster was the first BMW not to be fitted with a spare wheel: the car comes with a can of sealant and a compressor to pump the tire up.

The American-built Z3 has been dismissed by BMW's harsher critics as effete and awkwardly styled, but it is selling well. More butch versions like the M roadster have raised its credibility.

Few manufacturers had not explored each of these developments to some extent on their production vehicles and by the mid-1980s plastic moldings of one kind or another were to be found integrated into the body structure of most vehicles. The basic concept of course dated back to the mid-1950s Citroen DS and ID models and the Rover 2000 of the early 1960s. Both of these sedans used a skeleton body structure on which were hung nonstressed body panels. As a system it has its attractions, yet the claimed ease of accident repair is often illusory and there is a weight penalty along with the novel door arrangement. Yet despite a characteristically hefty price tag, the small numbers produced sold easily enough.

In the United Kingdom they cost £40,000 and seemed to move from BMW dealership to BMW dealership as novelty attractions. They were more rarely seen on the road and in retrospect, despite the claims that were made for them at the time, they had little long-term impact on BMW's subsequent development. The company and

press also made elaborate claims about the handling and levels of grip found on the Z1. Hindsight perhaps allows us to put these in perspective. To those used to the standard 3 series sedan, the new Z1 was a major improvement. The simple trailing arm layout that had been BMW's hallmark for many years was abandoned in favor of a more modern double wishbone layout with a degree of compliance built in to allow an element of rear-wheel steering. The result was a much more responsive car that also lost the roll oversteer typical of sedans. The company produced a total of 8,000 during the three-year production run and sold them in all the major BMW markets throughout the world

Its obvious successor, the commercially successful Z3, is no more than a competently designed two-seater derivative of the 3 series sedan. In spirit and engineering it bares the same relation to the 3 series that the United Kingdom volume sports cars of the mid-1960s and 1970s did to their parent sedans. Its success derives from its styling rather than its technical novelty, and the impetus for its production comes perhaps as much from the success of the MX3 Mazdas as it does BMW's experience with the Z1. In its later M version it delivers very high performance (though the M badge U.S.-spec cars are substantially tamer than those with the European M3 engine), but the car is regarded as somewhat effete in standard form. Some critics feel it is the first BMW for many years to genuinely miss the mark as a driver's car.

The Z3 is, of course, a genuine production model with none of the Z1 gimmicks or supposed novelties to increase production cost. Initially produced in BMW's new facility in South Carolina, its sales success meant that examples were subsequently produced in Germany. Both sales and profitability have been good and the Z3, though unlikely to be regarded as a classic, has been a useful adjunct to the range. U.S. sales alone amounted to around 90,000 between introduction in February 1996 and September 2000, with the 1.9 and 2.8 roadsters representing the bulk of the output. A curious and not entirely successful Z3 spin-off model—which certainly falls into the category of oddity—has been the M coupe, a three-door version cast in the cramped mold of the old MGB GT and Triumph GT6. BMW claimed that the M coupe was developed as a "spare time" project by enthusiastic Motorsport department engineers. This may well be characteristic marketing spin, but the car certainly stands apart from the tame open-topped Z3 versions, with its potent M-Power straight six delivering huge urge: with its old-style 1980s rear suspension (the chassis is based on the original Compact) it has something

The 3.2-liter engine gives 321 horsepower, but there was no space for the six-speed M3 gearbox. The top speed is limited to 154 miles per hour (the M roadster is poor aerodynamically, in any case) but the acceleration is truly wild: 0–60 in 5.4 seconds.

of the hard-edged appeal of the first of the M3s, which was clearly BMW's intention. Despite rave reviews from the enthusiast press, the Z3 coupe's prospective buyers seem resistant to its awkward styling, and as these words are written it probably hasn't much production life left.

BMW's latest profile-raising sports car, launched in the spring of 2000, is the Z8 roadster, styled in the image of the glamorous 1950s 507.

BMW's chief designer Chris Bangle called it, rather embarrassingly, a "retro car full of romantic passion." However, the links with BMW's rather tame 1950s flagship tend to hide the fact that this is an aggressive "driver's car" designed to straddle the chasm between sophisticated European exotica, such as the Porsche 911 and Ferrari 360 Modena, and more visceral hot rod machinery like the Dodge Viper. Its 5.0-liter, 400-horsepower V-8 engine is taken from the M5 sedan, and in this much lighter shell

Tail view shows the quad tail pipes and the optional roll hoops behind the seats.

The interior had a "retro" theme with chrome dials, twin tone leather, and red needles for the dials.

Cars like the M coupe prove that not even BMW gets it right every time. It's a great driver's car, but buyers have proved resistant to the unusual styling.

The Z8 is BMW's current glamour car and will only be produced in small numbers for a premium price. Styled to reflect the 507 of the 1950s, it is certainly more visually successful than the Z3.

Details like the 507-like wing vents, the slitty rear lights, and the split shark-nose grille give the Z8 great visual presence, though some think its looks rather kitsch and derivative.

The 5.0-liter, 32-valve 400-horsepower engine is borrowed from the current M5 saloon and in the much lighter Z8 provides outrageous performance—0–60 takes just 4.7 seconds.

Above: The interior is full of value-adding details and crafting, worlds away from the rational ergonomics of its mass-produced brethren.

To balance the enormous power, the Z8 features subtly effective stability and braking controls that interfere as little as possible with driver enjoyment.

delivers devastating urge, according to roadtesters. Its huge midrange acceleration is bettered only by Lamborghini's Diablo: 50–75 miles per hour in fourth takes 4.3 seconds in the Z8, which comes only with six-speed gearbox and a specification so complete that there are literally no options. The Z8 makes extensive use of light alloys for its aluminum space frame chassis (said to be exceptionally stiff), body panels and suspension, the latter being surprisingly free of sophisticated electronic aids.

When the hype has settled, the perspective on the car might not be so sunny: One has to wonder about the durability of its kitsch and derivative styling, which blends modern and 1950s rather clumsily in places. The interior looks fussy and self-conscious, especially from a company that has produced such rationally ergonomic dashboards in the past.

For an £84,000 car, of which only 8,000 are likely to be produced, it has earned its keep for BMW already in the number of column inches it has generated, true to the traditions of BMW's previous low-volume supercars. Journalists are still forming orderly queues for the chance to drive a Z8 and with such a limited production run, it is reasonable to assume that many of the cars will be bought by speculators and collectors.

THE 1990s:
NEW MODELS,
NEW MARKETS,
NEW DIRECTIONS

Previous page: the new E36 M3 was faster, smoother, and more refined than the car it replaced, but there was a feeling that it wasn't such a driver's car and had lost its edgy handling. Even so it sold well—70,000 units from 1993 to 1999.

The 1991 3 series was perhaps one of the most radical cars BMW has produced. The shape was daring after the extreme conformity of the long-lived E30 3 series, and it addressed aerodynamics and even recyclability—75 percent of the car could be reused. It set the standard for executive compacts through the 1990s.

BMW faced the 1990s with the strongest range of mainstream models—the 3 and 5 series—it had ever fielded. The new E36 3 series in particular was a dramatic departure from the car it replaced. Dr. Wolfgang Reitzle, BMW's research and development chief (who would later move to Ford and then Jaguar), said it was the biggest technology leap his company had ever made when it came to replacing one model with another.

Critics of the day said it needed to be, so aged and flawed was the outgoing model which, after all, had first seen the light of day eight years before. Outwardly the angular unforgiving lines of the old 3 series had been replaced by a design that many regarded as truly daring in 1990. With a bold twin kidney grille flanked by faired-in lights with an extremely short front overhang, it loudly proclaimed this was a rear- rather than front-wheel-drive machine. A front-drive prototype was built but dismissed on the grounds of torque-steer. There was also a version built with a Porsche 944–style rear transaxle for 50/50 weight distribution, but management rejected it because it intruded too much into the trunk space. Near 50/50 weight distribution was achieved anyway with the gearbox mounted conventionally.

The 0.32 drag coefficient of the 3 series was achieved by careful attention to below the beltline aerodynamics, with a flat undertray and a partially faired-in engine, plus more obvious external efforts like flush glass and low-drag door mirrors. The new shell offered 60 percent more torsional rigidity than its predecessor, was only marginally heavier, and offered much greater crash protection. There was talk, for the first time, about the recyclability of the car, an indication of the way green issues had exerted themselves on German politics in the 1980s. Seventy-five percent of the car, they said, could be recycled. Gearboxes were all new—the six-cylinder versions offered one of the first five-speed automatics—but the engine line-up was more familiar with the four-cylinder engines unchanged and the six-cylinders being the same 2.0- and 2.5-liter 24-valve units found in the 5 series.

New levels of sophistication were reached in the 3 series suspension, which used a version of the Z1's rear axle. Using so-called elastokinematic technology to keep

the wheels pointing in the most desirable direction, it was made up of kinked trailing arms pivoting on the same axes as the wheels and mounted in flexible rubber bushings. A pair of stacked track control arms were attached at right angles to the hub and were in turn linked to a four-point rear subframe in which the differential was elastically mounted. Clever bushing ensured that the wheels were relatively immune to bumps and lateral loading and braking forces, and BMW managed to make the car ride much better than the old model. The front suspension used an updated version of the old cars' spring and strut setup. Whatever the claims about a leap in technology, BMW retained its knack for choosing technological solutions that produced both appealing and profitable cars. It was this successful and delicate

balancing act that distinguished BMW once again from its competitors, rather than any leadership in technology.

Over the next few years, this third-generation 3 series would spawn not only a whole range of spin-off models—the Cabrio, Touring Estate, and M3 most memorably—but many imitators, such was the car's desirability. Despite the fact that there was a question mark over build quality on early examples (interior quality wasn't good, with air vents and door handles falling off, leading to a stream of warranty claims before the problems were cured) sales did not falter. The car became such an essential of the "lifestyle" of any young aspiring professional (or those who wanted to appear young, aspiring, and professional) that BMW could hardly produce the cars quick enough.

The two-door E36 3 series was easily the best-looking car BMW produced in the 1990s and became a best seller. Engines range from a frugal 318i to a 325 and, late in the run, a 328. All coupes came with door glasses that automatically dropped when the door opened to aid closure, a feature first seen on the 850i.

The new convertible 3 series was announced in the spring of 1993 and launched in the south of France. It was marginally heavier than its predecessor but, more importantly, 30 percent more rigid, and it featured a power top as standard. It was launched initially as a 325i; smaller-engined versions came later.

When the sleek two-door coupe version appeared, sales hardened even further and perhaps the only real challenger the car had during its lifetime was the new Audi A4, introduced in 1994. This car, front driven and ostensibly less "sporty" than the 3 series, to some extent benefited from the fact that the BMW 3 series was becoming a victim of its own success by the mid-1990s. There were so many of the cars on the road that the model—and indeed the marque—was no longer seen as exclusive. There was even a feeling abroad that BMW ownership was a tad vulgar: the Audi was marketed as a "thinking man's" alternative, a more tasteful, subtler choice.

Curiously BMW missed the mark when it came to producing a performance version of the 3 series, the new M3. This appeared in 1993 and was fast, refined, and made beautiful noises, but it lost the raw edge of excitement that had endeared the earlier four-cylinder model to enthusiasts. The reputation of the M3 badge wouldn't be reinstated until the new model was introduced in 2000. Moreover, the Japanese were set to make major inroads into the high-performance sedan market with four-wheel-drive turbocharged models that quickly set new performance and handling benchmarks.

The Compact was yet another 3 series spin-off announced in 1994 as a route into higher volume with a smaller, cheaper entry-level version. (Ironically, BMW had shortly beforehand absorbed Rover and bought into the volume range it hoped the Compact would give it entry to.) The Compact, available only with mild four-cylinder power, was built to appeal to buyers who were willing to abandon more lowly volume cars for the high "brand values" of a bargain basement BMW, no matter how basic the product in question might be. From the front it shared the wings and bonnet of the 3 series, but its stunted profile—it was 9 inches shorter than the standard

3 series, with a chopped-off tail and hatchback—hid drastically cheaper underpinnings. The trailing arm suspension was revived from the old-model 3 series, and the car felt much less stable through bumpy corners. The interior too was simplified in search of "sportiness" although it was really a cost-cutting exercise. Critics dismissed the car but it sold well enough to encourage BMW to produce a replacement in 2001, which was much more warmly received.

The 1988 5 series, while offering no technical novelty, was the darling of the motoring press and a vast improvement on the long-lived previous model, which

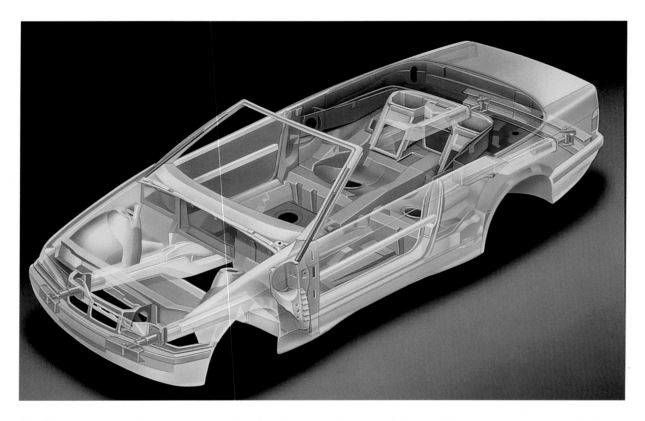

dated from 1972. Handsome, exceptionally refined and flattering of all levels of driving skill in its more potent forms, it was reckoned to be about the best buy in its class—perhaps the best all-round sedan in the world. Nothing else blended handling and ride comfort, performance and refinement quite so well, though the car had stiff competition from Mercedes' new E-Class and from a more unexpected quarter in Alfa's accomplished 164 V-6. Sadly, but perhaps predictably, the 164 appealed very much more to motoring journalists on its introduction than the cars do now to owners who find they have none of the BMW's longevity.

In style the 5 series was a cleverly down-scaled version of the 1985 7 series attributed to Claus Luthe, whose most famous previous design was the NSU R080. Indeed much of the suspension was carried over from the bigger car anyway, including a not entirely satisfactory form of electronic damper control. In refining a tried and tested technical formula, BMW produced a car with a much stiffer, substantially roomier, no lighter but slipperier bodyshell powered by a familiar range of six-cylinder engines ranging in capacity from 2.0 liters to 3.5 liters, the latter giving a top speed of over 140 miles per hour. High gearing in the name of economy

highlighted the lack of ultimate torque, even in the bigger-engined version, but the company would address this in later years in the 4.0-liter 540, using the new V-8.

For aggressive drivers, the best news of all came in the form of the new M5, the fastest four-door sedan in the world (electronically limited to 156 miles per hour but good for 170 when derestricted) and powered by what many regarded as the world's finest six-cylinder engine, the twin-cam 24-valve unit now giving 314 horsepower. There were faster, better-looking performance cars, said the pundits, but nothing did a combination of things so well as this still modest-looking five-seater BMW.

Acquisition or "Brand-Stretching": The Rover Debacle

BMW in the 1990s clearly sought to build upon its achievements. Acknowledged as the benchmark for vehicle design and quality, and with a brand image envied by all other manufacturers, it sought to capitalize on its position by extending the range of vehicles that it produced.

Any company in a competitive economy must always seek new opportunity and respond to change. BMW recognized the growth in vehicle numbers would be limited in the sector in which it operated. BMW already claimed a major slice of the sports and luxury market worldwide, and supported this position by making less well-specified models for the German home market in large numbers. Yet to maintain the pace of growth that it had achieved, and to produce the kind of financial security and performance that its shareholders required, the company explored new sectors of the market, as did other luxury carmakers. For BMW though, it presented a problem. Did it carry its own brand name downmarket, with the obvious dangers that could arise, or did it seek a merger or partnership with a volume producer?

The motor industry was consolidating globally with a wave of mergers, acquisitions and partnerships, and a certain competitive edge had become associated with exploring merger and acquisition opportunity. Such activity became the public symbol of a successful company. German industry in general had gone through successive waves of overseas acquisition, though many of them had proved unsuccessful. On the other hand, a new generation of German managers saw themselves as less conservative and more international in their outlook. For them, the global merger and acquisition activity that characterized international business had a real appeal.

What little was left of the United Kingdom motor industry presented itself as obvious targets. BMW made several forays into the United Kingdom, competing with VW in a rather farcical contest to secure

This 318i was the first car to be produced by BMW's Spartanburg factory in South Carolina. All the people responsible for building the car and setting up the factory signed it.

The E34-based M5, although as understated in appearance as its predecessors, was easily the best high-performance sedan in the world. It retained the Motorsport straight six, now with 315 horsepower and a slightly larger capacity of 3,535 cc. The car could reach 60 from rest in 6.3 seconds and had a top speed electronically limited to 155 miles per hour. Later, a bigger 3.8-liter 340-horsepower engine was introduced, and in 1994 a six-speed gearbox. These cars were hand-assembled and are very desirable used buys.

Rolls-Royce/Bentley, which was offered for sale, along with engine manufacturer Cosworth, by the existing owners, Vickers Group. BMW was the preferred buyer, as it already had strong links with the company through an agreement to supply its V-8 and V-12 engines for both the Rolls and Bentley models. It made sense for BMW as a leading luxury carmaker to associate itself with Rolls and Bentley, while the smaller company could no longer afford the development costs for new engines.

This arrangement was disrupted by VW-Audi, which was also on the acquisition trail. VW outbid BMW, only to find that purchase of the company did not bring with it acquisition of the Rolls-Royce name. Those rights were acquired by BMW which, in turn, refused to continue supplying BMW engines following VW's acquisition. This left VW in the awkward position of having to try to secure the rights to the name through European Community law, as well as to devise a replacement for BMW's engines. Not surprisingly, VW was forced into an agreement by which BMW would acquire Rolls-Royce in a couple of years time, along with the rights to the "spirit of ecstasy" mascot and trading name, while VW would retain Bentley. BMW could represent

the deal as a victory, but in business terms it is perhaps of limited significance.

The acquisition of Rover was a bigger deal and presented a greater challenge. Ultimately it was an acquisition that made the company look rather foolish and dented its reputation for business acumen. BMW was usually the case study used in business schools worldwide to illustrate success, achievement, and best practice. In the case of the Rover debacle, it became the favorite case study of strategic failure. The logic behind the acquisition was simple enough: BMW wished to broaden its base and use its talents to generate income from further down the market without tainting the BMW brand. Rover was one of the few volume producers readily available for acquisition, and within Rover group was the highly successful Land Rover, which had been the market leader in 4x4 vehicles for many decades. While commentators speak of access to Land Rover technology and expertise as a motivation for the merger, given BMW's recognition that the development of sport utility vehicles (SUVs) and 4x4s offered new opportunity in the United States, this seems unlikely. There is little doubt that BMW would have had little difficulty developing vehicles of this kind from its own resources.

What did appeal was the Land Rover operation's profitability and its associations of brand leadership within the sector. BMW also seemed to have been curiously attracted to the Mini and to have seen it as an important part of the group's future. In some ways this is understandable, as BMW was otherwise without any presence in the small-car market and environmental concerns suggested this could be a growth area in the future, albeit with the inevitable difficulties of generating sufficient margins on small cars.

Whatever the reasoning, BMW competed with Honda in the acquisition of the Rover group, despite the fact that virtually all the Rover group cars were based on slightly outdated Honda models. Honda had also worked comparatively successfully in conjunction with the British company, raising levels of quality and, for the first time in many years making the Rover group moderately stable and successful—so much so that British Aerospace, which had acquired Rover some years earlier, was in a position to sell Rover off to its financial advantage. British Aerospace chose to do this rather than face the necessary investment that would be required to update the product line.

Once BMW acquired the Rover Group, it seemed to devote little interest in managing its acquisition. Most commentators remark on its surprising hands-off approach to the British company. Local management was seemingly left undisturbed for three to four years. Only when the losses mounted dramatically were German managers introduced and detailed controls modeled on the practice in Munich introduced. Perhaps more important than the origins of the management was the fact the BMW failed early on to establish a strategy that would shape Rover's future. With the links to Honda severed, and the need to develop new vehicle platforms if Rover was to remain a volume car producer, the future of the venture looked uncertain from quite early on.

At the same time, Rover's export performance was severely handicapped by the increasing exchange value of the pound, which undermined its competitiveness in export markets. Losses mounted, and there did not seem to be an obvious way out of the situation. Rover's plant lacked the level of investment to generate the necessary levels of productivity. It is hard to describe it as a well-managed episode in BMW's recent history, and it certainly is the case that it coincided with, or generated, strong internal dissension among the company's senior executives. Some have suggested that BMW's then-executive chairman,

Bernd Pischetsrieder, had an emotional attachment to the BMW-Rover deal. Whatever the reality, he was sufficiently closely associated with the policies adopted that he was to lose his job as a result. He quickly found his way to VW-Audi.

The supervisory board, controlled by the Quandt family, addressed the matter in characteristic BMW style in the spring of 2000. Losses had mounted and the enthusiasm for global acquisition adventures had diminished. Rover was to be disposed of as soon as possible at whatever cost. The scale of the problem was perhaps always overestimated by United Kingdom–focused media. BMW was a large enough company, and was securely enough rooted, to accommodate errors even on this scale. Nevertheless, it was a blow to BMW's pride and image.

For the future BMW has pledged itself to continued independent growth. The company itself has always been a possible target for takeover from the industry giants. Ford has always shown a keen interest in the company and every so often rumors link Volkswagen with BMW. Yet after the Rover fiasco, CEO Joachim Milburg outlined to shareholders the plan for the future. "We will pursue a strategy based on the BMW brand extending from the lower midrange segment all the way to the luxury-performance segment." Rejecting mergers as a route to a larger role for BMW, Milburg argued that "the BMW Group will continue to grow under its own

Those who required something a bit less aggressive could choose one of the new V-8-engined 5 series models, the 530 and 540i. First seen in the 7 series in 1992, the V-8 replaced the old 3.5-liter straight six and was BMW's first V-8 design since the demise of the 3200 coupes and saloons in the early 1960s. Light for their size, they were exceptionally smooth. The power and refinement of the 4.0-liter version made the V-12 BMW seem rather redundant.

The 7 series entered its third generation in 1994. The styling was a tasteful, cautious update of the previous one, rather than a radical departure, but under the skin it really was all new, aside from the V-8 and V-12 engines. It faced new opposition from the four-wheel-drive Audi A8.

power, without requiring any mergers or diversification." It will build an entry-level compact under the BMW brand, having now rejected the strategy that led it to purchase Rover. Its objective now is to produce higher-volume cars under the BMW name without impacting adversely on the core business.

In a vision of the future very different from the neat three-model line-up of the last couple of decades, BMW now looks as though it will be represented at virtually every level of the market. BMW hopes that a brand stretching exercise will allow it to have vehicles in every sector, from the small front-wheel-drive car—launched in the spring of 2001 as the new Mini—to BMW's interpretation of the Rolls-Royce heritage. In between these extremes its traditional representation in the sports-luxury market is as strong as ever, but now also includes the four-wheel-drive SUV X5 model that has received a very positive welcome from testers and the public alike. Designed and built in North America (alongside the Z3

at Spartanburg, South Carolina) the X5 was introduced in 2000 as a rival to Mercedes' M-Class, which is also U.S. built, the Americans having a seemingly insatiable appetite for 4x4 vehicles.

To its credit the X5 doesn't look as vulgar as many of its ilk and on-road is likely to be the best driving of all, its carlike handling being little different, say testers, from a 5 series Touring. Off-road, it is capable rather than outstanding, lacking differential locks or a high- and low-ratio gearbox. BMW feels its automatic stability control should be good enough for most drivers' off-road requirements, an acknowledgment that the X5 will rarely venture onto rough terrain. The fact that it uses unitary construction rather than a chassis (as is still the convention in the SUV world) seems to be the main reason for its good handling. It is also exceptionally fast for an off-roader. In V-8 sport form it will easily top 140 miles per hour, although nonsport versions are limited to 128.

More Laurels for the 3 and 5 Series and a Much Improved Compact

The new 1995 5 series built on BMW's reputation for making the best midrange sedan in the business. Subsequent challengers like the Jaguar S-Type (which was benchmarked against the 5 series during its development), Mercedes E-Class, and Audi A6 have somehow failed to topple the BMW's claim to being the leading car in its class, with a ride and handling compromise that is probably not bettered by any car in the world, regardless of price. Technically the basics were much as before—only turbo-diesel engines and transmissions were carried over—but in detail the car was entirely new from the floorpan upward, and BMW made much play of its extensive use of lightweight steels, aluminum, and computer-aided design technology to produce a car that was stiffer and, for the first time, lighter than the model that preceded it. Even the basic 2.0-liter model could now top 130 miles per hour

and the 4.0-liter V-8 version seemed almost excessively potent for what was, after all, a comfortable executive express. The styling, while bold and chunky at the front, seemed to fizzle out into blandness at the rear. Yet the shape has served BMW well and still looks thoroughly contemporary as these words are written, almost six years on from its introduction. In customary style, critics dribbled over the shatteringly fast M5 version that appeared in autumn 1998, which mixed supercar power delivery and sharp handling while remaining as docile and usable as the basic 2.0-liter version.

For those who needed less sheer power, perhaps the best all-rounder of all was the handsome 330d Touring. Here was a spacious 140-mile-per-hour, 40-mile-per-gallon estate car fitted with BMW's superbly torquey turbo-diesel straight six. The day of the performance diesel had arrived, and BMW was in the vanguard of development with a power unit that made buyers question the need to ever buy another gasoline-engined executive car.

The X5 is one of the best of the current-generation SUVs and an amazingly good first attempt for BMW in this specialized market. Powered by a 4.0-liter V-8 or 3.0-liter six-cylinder gasoline engine, or a 3.0-liter diesel, the X5 drives on the road like a 5 series sedan.

In the savagely fought compact executive stakes, the 1998 fourth-generation 3 series maintained its position, but the opposition was much more aggressive than ever before. Alfa Romeo had a genuine challenger for the first time in the elegant 156, which some regarded as a more rewarding driver's car, despite its front-wheel drive. Rear drive maintained the 3 series spiritual and technical link with more expensive BMW models in a sector that was dominated by front drivers. It was essentially a down-scaled 5 series in both its visuals and engineering, and BMW achieved its design objectives in producing a 3 series that was roomier, safer, and better equipped than the one that came before. On the downside, it was felt BMW had injected so much refinement that the car lost a little of its edge in the driver appeal stakes, though its huge competence was never in doubt.

More worryingly, buyers were beginning to voice nagging doubts about the sheer ubiquity of the 3 series and the kinds of people who were driving them. What had once been a car for well-heeled individualists was now seen as something of an unimaginative choice. Customers who thought themselves true connoisseurs perhaps bought an Alfa or an Audi, conscious that it didn't carry with it the brash contentions that seemed to haunt BMW more doggedly with each successive new model. In terms of image, the 3 series *was* becoming a victim of its own success. In its promotion of the car, BMW sought desperately, but subtly, to reassure its constituency that it still made cars for educated professionals, not South London gangsters.

Spanning 35 variants, the 3 series range was topped in 2001 by the new M3, a six-speed, 348-horse-power powerhouse that successfully blended the overt sophistication of the 1993 model (which had sold a healthy 71,000 units) with the raw aggression of the original four-cylinder M3. In looks it evoked something of the elegance of the CSL coupe of the 1970s and provided a blistering drive, overshadowing even the M5 for sheer excitement.

In all this excitement, the 7 series had been rather forgotten. To some observers it seemed that BMW didn't take its flagship model very seriously, because the volume of sales was relatively low, leaving it to Mercedes to produce the truly outstanding German limousine with its S-Class. Introduced in 1994, the third-generation 7 series was an excellent car that actually sold tolerably well, but unless you truly needed its extra generous rear legroom and every last power-assisted aid to luxury, many felt the 5 series did the job just as well for less money. For its size, it was an unusually rewarding car to

drive, but the flagship V-12 750 model seemed rather pointless when the 740 was so smooth and fast, and it felt too much like less-expensive BMWs to have appeal as a true plutocrat's limousine.

Models for the Future

The new century has seen BMW continue its policy of updating its offerings. In 2001 a new version of the Compact was introduced. Mindful of the criticisms leveled at the earlier model, BMW made sure its new entry was technically contemporary in every respect with the 3 series: no botched-up rear suspension this time. Two engine sizes were offered, a clever 1.6 with a "Valvetronic" throttle system (claimed to clean up emissions and reduce fuel consumption) and a top-of-the-range 325Ti six-cylinder. Built to take on Audi's accomplished A3, BMW's Compact was not an austerity model that would only be bought by people who couldn't afford a full-size 3 series, but a car with a separate identity of its own. Pundits in the United Kingdom were not so sure, and pointed out that for an entry-level car with very little rear legroom, it was exceedingly pricey—the 325Ti was £3,000 more than a 4-Motion four-wheel-drive VW Golf.

As this book is in preparation, a new-generation 7 series has been shown to, but not driven by, the press. It will be unveiled at the Frankfurt International Motor Show in September 2001. Styled by Chris Bangle, it is perhaps the most visually controversial BMW since the first seven series of 1977, a large bloated car with slabby flanks and a fat roofline. Powered by heavily revised versions of BMW's established V-8s and eventually a V-12, it seems certain to be an impressive car to drive. It will be intriguing to see how well the optional "active" air suspension will work. The interior is a radical departure from established BMW practice, with the controls for its luxury features boiled down to just a few multifunction stalks in what BMW calls its iDrive system. The transmission selector—operating the world's first six-speed automatic—is a stalk on the steering column. Mounted where you'd expect to find the gear lever is a circular knob controlling climate, music, navigation, and an onboard Internet link.

Yet the new models' lauded features and the customary acclaim with which they are greeted by the motoring press cannot obscure the challenges faced by BMW in the new century. Whether BMW will be able to manage its brand in such a way that it retains dominance while being represented in the proposed newly diverse market sectors remains an open question. In business, perhaps especially auto business, dominant leadership can quickly be eroded. To stay strong, leading manufacturers must constantly respond to new competitors and changes in fashion and popular aspiration.

Part of BMW's motivation to explore other market segments has been the arrival of Japanese manufacturers in the luxury high-performance sector in the 1990s. In the area of performance cars, Subaru and Mitsubishi are successful newcomers that a decade ago had very little impact in this sector. Lexus and Infiniti have also made serious initial inroads into the luxury-car market, though they seem now to have difficulty sustaining an impact. On the other hand, Jaguar, backed by Ford's resources, is set to significantly increase production volumes with the X-type—aimed squarely at traditional BMW customers. Lexus with its IS200, a competitive if slightly garish car, is also clearly targeting BMW's mainstay 3 and 5 series models.

Yet BMW has had no difficulty dealing with competition in the past and has displayed a remarkable stability and assurance in its strategy. As a business, BMW has shown for four decades the ability to meet challenges.

Just as nation states invent and reshape their histories to reinforce their sense of purpose, so BMW has projected and shaped our vision of its history as an integral part of its marketing. In the 1990s it reaped the rewards of this consistency, becoming the benchmark for those seeking to define quality and performance.

BMW's success has reflected an age where growing affluence has been accompanied by great sensitivity to possessions as defining individuality.

Over the last three or four decades, social status has shifted from an accident of birth to something individuals define by what they possess. Though different parts of the world have experienced these changes in different ways and to different degrees, there has been no doubt that BMW could market products that spoke to the aspirations of vast numbers of people across national boundaries.

For all the talk of technologies and functionality, the appeal of cars in recent decades has been sensual and aesthetic. BMW's strength has been its ability to make profitable cars which, whatever their failings, always had some flair and distinction. They were in tune with their times, which was often much more important than being at the forefront in technology. The company's ability to plan, learn, and adapt within an ever-changing market environment has been impressive. But business cultures are changing and becoming more global. The distinctive industrial environment of postwar Germany, and the sustained economic boom

with which it is associated, are all now part of history. Will BMW be able to adapt yet again to a changing world and maintain its dominance?

Whether twenty-first-century customers will value the same things, be responsive to the same cultural cues, and share the same aspirations, remains an open question. A new generation usually rejects the fashions and choices of its parents. BMW as much as anyone has played its part in making cars fashion items and subtle social statements. Perhaps the new generation of twenty-first-century customers will not meet BMW's offerings with the same eagerness that the company has come to expect. BMW may find that its current success could be its greatest burden in the future. Whatever may happen, the current generation of motoring enthusiasts can be grateful for the legacy of fine cars the company created and the leadership it gave to the industry.

The X5 under construction at BMW's American Spartanburg factory. The vehicle's styling is more agreeable than many of its ilk, and BMW is struggling to keep pace with demand.

INDEX